The Shared Wisdom of Mothers and Daughters

The Shared Wisdom of Mothers and Daughters

The Timelessness of Simple Truths

Alexandra Stoddard

WILLIAM MORROW

An Imprint of HarperCollins*Publishers*

HarperCollins books may be purchased for educational, business, or sales promotional use. For information please write: Special Markets Department, HarperCollins Publishers, 10 East 53rd Street, New York, NY 10022.

FIRST EDITION

Library of Congress Cataloging-in-Publication Data has been applied for.

ISBN 978-0-06-211637-6

13 14 15 16 17   ov/rrd   10 9 8 7 6 5 4 3 2 1

To my beloved daughters, Alexandra and Brooke.
I am continuously proud of you and blessed to be your mother.
You bring me great love, joy, pleasure, happiness, wisdom,
and inspiration every day.

Live within the present,
without regretting, fearing,
or hoping for anything.

—PIERRE HADOT

Contents

Preface

When my daughters were young, my duty as their mother was to teach them things I thought they should know. It was not entirely a one-way street, but certainly the responsibility was weighted on my side. As time passed, I found that things I wanted to teach them were often enriched by their own insights. The balance of who was teaching whom became more even.

This new book is a mixture of things I feel are important to tell my daughters and things they want me to know. The wonderful reality is that almost none of this is purely one-sided—with the exception of my aversion to technology! Most of these essays reflect a merger of minds and hearts, and, because of the evolution that has transpired, this book's point of view is wider and deeper than that of *Things I Want My Daughters to Know*. I have been incredibly moved by the shared wisdom we have acquired as we've matured.

One of my gifts to my daughters and my readers is my thirst for knowledge. The lives of great thinkers through the ages are rich and insightful, and I want to share their teachings through my own prism so you can apply these lessons in your own life. I feel a strong desire to express some of the powerful forces that have shaped mine. Sharing the wisdom of the brilliant minds I've studied over the past forty-five years is deeply satisfying to me, and I treasure this opportunity to pass their words along to my daughters and my readers.

One of the most important lessons I want to teach my daughters is to grow old vigorously—continuously stretching their minds—and to remain vitally engaged in a full, generous, and happy life.

1

....

Embrace the Changing Balance
in Your Relationship

Your whole past was but a birth and a becoming.

*Grown-ups never understand anything for themselves, and it is tiresome
for children to be always and forever explaining things to them.*

—*Antoine de Saint-Exupéry*

When I wrote *Things I Want My Daughters to Know*, my daughters, Alexandra and Brooke, were young adults. Now they are middle-aged! Even then, as I shared in my essay "Listen to the Wisdom of Your Children," I paid attention to my daughters, and found their company more stimulating than that of many of our friends. Their evolving wisdom and our growing love for one another is profound.

Of course, the love parents share with their offspring is a different kind of bond than that shared with a best friend from college, but it can be a closeness and mutual respect that is solid over all the years. When

Alexandra and Brooke speak to me, I take what they say seriously. On their advice, I bought our cottage, and when we sold our apartment in New York City, they persuaded us not to buy another apartment in the city but to live in Connecticut full-time. I am strongly influenced by their advice and teachings, their thoughtfulness and concerns. Since we don't always think the same way, my daughters and I are able to learn from one another new ideas that can open our minds to thinking with an illuminated perspective and help us to do things differently. I have a tendency to not like to hear sad news. Occasionally, when Alexandra or Brooke has something serious to tell me, they'll suggest that I listen and really hear what they're saying.

Everyone who knows me understands how I feel about motherhood. I loved raising my daughters and had fun. Looking back, I feel I was a natural mother because I enjoyed being with them. We did interesting things together in the city and on our international trips every August.

A few years ago, we were all together for Thanksgiving, in Maryland, at Alexandra's house. As the banquet was being prepared, I was playing games with and losing badly to my whip-smart grandchildren. Brooke's daughter, Cooper, was walking her stuffed animals in a baby stroller. My husband, Peter, was seated in his favorite chair in the sunroom, petting Alexandra's family's golden retriever, Homer. As I looked around, seeing a beautifully set table, gleaming silverware, sparkling clean glasses, and flowers in abundance, a sudden realization jolted me from my reverie while I was adoring my family: this moment was a dream come true.

I revere my daughters and grandchildren, and to see them living so well, with order, beauty, rituals, and celebrations, made me acutely aware that now, when we are together as a family, we cover four generations with an age spread of eighty-seven years. Even though this process has been a gradual revelation, it dawned on me completely, at that exact moment, that our relationship now reflects a wonderful change, from maternal to the best kind of mutual love, caring, respect, and friendship. My heart was bursting with pride and honor. All these years of my taking care of my daughters have ever so gradually evolved into their not only taking care of themselves and their families but also being able to advise my husband and me as we grow older.

I know for certain that Alexandra and Brooke have solidly good values, and if I were to give them advice about their lives, I'd praise them for their character and how they conduct themselves, encouraging them to carry on as they are doing and cling to their unwavering principles.

The times we are together are precious moments I treasure and store safely in my memory bank to draw on when we're not face-to-face. What's especially poignant and lovely is how these times together with my grown daughters' children echo the joy I felt as a young mother raising my daughters themselves. Having the blessings of grandchildren is like going back in time and getting caught up in the joy all over again. The stark difference between being a mother and being a grandmother is that the mother has all the heartaches and worries and does all the hard work. I'm now allowed to play around with the grands. What could be a greater gift?

I melt when a granddaughter wants to sit next to me at a meal, the way my daughters did when they were young. Alexandra and Brooke would trade places for dessert. I marvel at children's affection for their parents and grandparents. I tried not to spoil my daughters, but when I became a grandmother I stopped trying. My grandchildren are too precious for words.

This gradual evolution from a point where we had a hierarchical status to one where we share insights and wisdom has been richly rewarding. My daughters and I are now on an equal playing field; what was once vertical is now horizontal. Together we have bridged the divide. There is a parallelism here of our coming together to help one another. These two adult women, who happen to be my loving daughters, are just as concerned that I have a happy and fulfilling life as I am interested that they do.

Over the years they have taught me new insights about their generation, cultural matters, politics, and the toys of modern civilization, as well as the pace of modern life. So often, I think of something in a new way because of an insight they've shared with me. Their lessons are sharp, often funny, and wise. These young women know things my husband and I don't, and I find it moving that they care enough to share their education and information with us. Their advice is never demeaning but always profoundly helpful.

After all, when people love us, they tell us not only what we want to hear but what we need to know. Who knows me better than my daughters? They have the informed perspective to continually make intelligent recommendations. We developed and grew into this ongoing, reciprocal relationship that is a source of great strength and support to Peter and me. As we mature, we evolve and grow, learning from everything around us. No matter how old I am, I will always have more to share with my daughters and will look for ways to be useful to them. This balance of give and take, teaching and learning, helping and receiving help, gives us mutual confidence and hope.

All of the events in our lives have led to an expansion of knowledge. I have an open mind and an open heart as I am continually learning from the great minds throughout history, my readers, my audiences, my daughters, and, indeed, everyone I meet. I haven't stopped growing now that my daughters have reached maturity, nor have they. Our intellectual bank account keeps expanding.

My daughters' contributions to my understanding and point of view are profound. What a blessing it is to have this wisdom go both ways. From the things they are trying to teach me I have learned how smart and wise they are, making this a delightful exchange, a two-way street where our love and understanding grow each year.

I hope some of the remarkable insights my daughters have given me will prove as valuable to my readers as they have been to me. A friend sent me a letter her mother wrote her that she said was the most beautiful letter she had ever read:

> *My Dearest Paulette, Daughter,*
> *It is 3:27 A.M. the day we call Memorial Day. I have just finished* Traveling with Pomegranates. *I can really understand why you loved it so. I think my favorite lines are "It's the channel where the souls of a mother and a daughter open and flow as two separate adults, woman to woman. It is, I know now, a place created through necessary loss and necessary search and a reinvention of the whole relationship."*
>
> —SUE MONK KIDD

> *It is for me, the time to tell you just how proud I am of you as a mother, wife, daughter and you as a person. I am at peace knowing you will be able to handle anything that comes your way.*

So our relationship has been "reinvented"! It truly is on a different
level woman to woman—the child I loved so is gone—grown into a
woman I love even more. If I died tomorrow—my soul can rest in
peace for you.
The night now is dark and very still—very misty, lots of fog;
good for the spirits to travel through! I'm not doing anything
today (Monday) that I don't want to do. I would love to hug you!
Although physically we are far apart we are so fortunate because
for us the bond between mother and daughter is unquestioned and
unyielding. Just a message from one woman to another.

Love, Mom, Charlene

The dynamics of our relationship have changed. We are now communicating person to person. The more my daughters feel happy, free, fulfilled, and unrestrained in their lives, the greater my joy. My love and respect for them have no bounds. If I sound like an adoring mother, this is a fact, and my words are the truth.

I will continue to embrace the changing balance in our relationship all my life with sincere gratitude for the devotion we share.

Never on any account . . . allow any hostility to grow up between yourself and
a child.

—Maxwell Perkins

2

Cultivate the Ideal
Pleasure of Everyday Life

Hurry up and live, and consider each day as a completed life. . . .
He who believes every day that his life has been complete enjoys
peace of mind.

He enjoys the present without depending on what does not yet exist. . . .
He does not hurl himself toward an uncertain goal, for he is satisfied with
what he has. Nor is he satisfied with little, for what he possesses is in the
universe. . . . "All this belongs to me."

—Seneca

Balance is the essential ingredient for a good life. When we are balanced, we are mentally, psychologically, and emotionally stable, prerequisites for lasting happiness.

In order to achieve a state of equilibrium, a harmonious whole, we have to cultivate the grace of inner peace and contentment available to us.

Why is it that many of us resist lifestyle adjustments that would improve our health and well-being? Why can't we move toward our center now and form good habits in our daily lives in order to find more ways to seek greater value and meaning before there is a crisis? Living well requires great thoughtfulness in being able to achieve this internal balance and sustain it over time.

Everyone wants to find more pleasure in their everyday life. While I'm alive I want to feel radiant and vital. I want to feel the rapture of being alive that Joseph Campbell wrote about. I want to follow my bliss. I want to experience the wonder of possibilities. I want to become well adjusted, spending as much time as possible being fully engaged in all the simple daily pleasures that I know from experience will feed my soul.

I love my daily rituals and take enormous pleasure in the process of almost everything I do. Even the little things I'd rather not do—like shooing an irritating buzzing fly out the window of my writing room—I do, because all of them are for my own benefit. I'm determined to make things work out as well as humanly possible, no matter what the outer circumstances. For me, it is a matter of pride and self-respect that, for the most part, I'm able to control myself. And while I try to understand my limitations, I'm also aware of my strengths. I have a burning desire to live an orderly life of integrity rather than the alternative of chaos and mindless superficiality.

Many diverse factors play key roles in how we balance our inner lives. In order to even dream of the ideal pleasure of everyday life, we need to identify our core values and uphold the standards that support our even keel and inner calm. In order to strike a judicious balance, we need to become more open-minded and less judgmental and to acquire the skill of being reasonable, of being able to see the big picture from all the different points of view. Nothing is as simple as black and white or yes and no. Everything has shades of gray, and the brighter the sunlight the deeper the shadow.

I am extremely empathetic to the masses of people who are dissatisfied with their lives. But it is only intelligent to appreciate what we have and continuously seek and find the deeper significance from the humble, caring, quiet, often unrecognized daily activities we perform.

It's amazing how the Golden Rule helps me remember that we should try never to do something to someone that we would not want done to us. While we all appreciate our great freedom and flexibility, being able to follow our own schedules is crucial to our ability to function well. While we all have the need to be open to others, because that is the essence of life in the human society, we should be wary of being too open. We all need doors to close and need to have others respect our boundaries without our having to explain ourselves.

The more we know and understand our own needs, the better we'll be at acting appropriately with others. Our intuitive perception will increase our own awareness of a situation. We will have a visceral feeling, sensing what is the best way to act. Intuition is our sixth sense, making us more sensitive in our interactions with others. Love is paradoxical because sometimes it is most thoughtful to leave people alone. Most of us want more privacy and time by ourselves than we have; this is especially true of parents. We all, especially caregivers, have many people who depend on us. All of us sometimes want and need to just walk away to clear our heads.

I can only imagine, after she's made all the necessary arrangements for her family, how luxurious it must feel for my daughter Alexandra to fly alone to New Orleans to see her best friend, temporarily leaving behind her husband, children, dog, and work. Everyone needs a break from their daily responsibilities, constant interruptions, and other people's demands on their time.

Whenever I fly or take a train, I bury myself in my work. I don't make eye contact with the people I'm squeezed up against. This is *my* time, and I carefully guard it.

Alexandra always looks forward to walking her dog, Homer. Sometimes she is joined by her children, but she really needs this time to think and to be in her own company, free from obligations to others. If Alexandra doesn't invite someone to join her on her walk or an errand, it is because she wants to be alone. In an overwhelmingly crowded schedule, these mini escapes are essential to her well-being. When we plan our time wisely and we look forward to something, and anticipate it, we deserve to see to it that we follow through with our plan.

Alexandra's children adore Aunt Brookie and can't get enough of her when we're all visiting. They want to sit next to her at meals and spend all their time with her when they can. One morning when Brooke popped up to run to Tom's News Stand, Nicholas, Anna, and Lily wanted to go, too. Alexandra explained to her children that once you're a mother, sometimes, no matter how much you love everyone, you crave a moment's peace and want to be alone. We can all identify with this feeling. And there are times when a few moments here and a few moments there may not be enough.

Healthy boundaries go both ways. Respecting the wishes of those whom we care most about makes for mutual satisfaction in a loving relationship. I remember one Easter when Alexandra canceled coming to

Peter's and my cottage in Stonington, Connecticut, because she had a cat that was dying. Not everyone is a cat lover, but a cat lover would never leave a dying cat. This is a good example of having healthy boundaries. Obviously, Alexandra knew that I'd be disappointed, but she also knew how much she needed to take care of her sweet cat, Lesieur. I have such respect for her doing the right thing under the circumstances.

Sometimes, we are the ones who have to disappoint other people's plans. Often their expectations can be more imaginary than realistic. In social situations and especially when family is involved, a great deal of diplomacy is required in order not to hurt people's feelings, while not doing something that isn't the right fit for you at the time. All of us bend over backward for others at certain times in our lives and are able to make loving sacrifices, especially in periods of celebration, crisis, or illness. Most of us make an effort to please others, but sometimes people try to put demands on us that would be inappropriate or disrupt our own well-thought-out decisions, made on the basis of information we choose not to share with them. There is no reason we should have to explain the details of our circumstances. You can't possibly plan your life with any intelligence and integrity if you overextend yourself.

There is so much about all of our lives that appropriately should remain private. We should not feel under any obligation to explain all the graphic details of our specific situations. The pressure we feel should be the demands we put on ourselves, not the commands of others.

There has to be an invisible line we draw in the sand where we ourselves don't cross over and won't allow others to overstep. We are all striving to gain more control over ourselves and learn how to put our time to the most rewarding use. This, of course, is an evolving process. When we do arrive at a state of personal awareness, we want to do whatever it takes to sustain this sense of equilibrium, knowing how fragile we can be when we extend ourselves beyond what feels comfortable or is healthy.

Think of having an inner scale where you weigh your decisions—and base them not on your calendar and your ability to physically do something, but on what the inner scale tells you. You should always consider the emotional consequences—how much stress and disruption an event will cause you. Think carefully as well about your sense of responsibility to yourself. It is vitally important to maintain a healthy balance between overextending yourself for others and taking care of your personal needs, like regularly carving out time to do meaningful work you love. Remember, you are in charge of how you spend your time.

I have a plastic ring with a Day-Glo green carpenter's level in it that I keep on my desk. I put it on my little finger and fidget with it, shifting the bubble from one end to the other and then back into the center, but it doesn't stay still. Any slight movement to the right or left moves the bubble away from being level. This silly little toy is a welcome distraction as I try to be levelheaded about the way I conduct my daily life. The undulating bubble is a reminder that when I'm in control of myself, when I'm in charge of what commitments I make to others based on my ever-changing, invisible inner scale, I will be living from my center. This, for all of us, is the goal. I've found that when we're unrealistic about our limitations, the smallest thing can make that bubble move from the ideal balance to an extreme away from the middle.

Ever since I can remember, I have been extremely sensitive to my surroundings. Feng shui, the ancient Chinese art and practice of positioning objects (especially graves, buildings, and furniture), is based on a belief in patterns of yin and yang that balance the flow of our vital energy, ch'i, which has positive and negative effects. *Feng* is wind; *shui*, water. Master feng shui practitioners teach us that we are constantly in relationship to the positive energy in our paths and must always be doing what we want to do in order to flourish.

It is possible for each of us to create an ideal environment in order to be able to fulfill our potential with faith, confidence, and integrity, focusing on what we desire to achieve and how we choose to live. After we know what is the best environment for us to not merely cope, but thrive in, we have to honor what we understand is best, in our ever-changing circumstances, in order to be at our best in everything we hold dear.

Each of us decides what is right for us in our current environment, and then we have to make a leap of faith to believe in ourselves sufficiently to be strong enough to follow through with our insights.

We have a long way to go, but we'll be headed in a kinder, more loving direction when we strive for our own balance and learn how to sustain it, knowing just how difficult it is to bring this inner scale to equilibrium.

Michel de Montaigne teaches us how to become more mindful:

When I dance, I dance; when I sleep, I sleep; yes, and when I walk alone in a beautiful orchard, if my thoughts have been dwelling on extraneous incidents for some part of the time, for some other part I bring them back to the walk, to the orchard, to the sweetness of this solitude, and to me.

We have to monitor our attitude constantly, moment by moment. Are we acting out of love and appreciation or guilt, resentment, and frustration? How able are we to direct our thoughts where they are most appropriate? How often are we too afraid to do the things we want to do in order to become the people we choose to be, hesitating out of fear of failing or having others criticize us? If our frame of mind is anxious, we will not be true to ourselves, or able to think reasonably about anything. Remember the humor of Mark Twain: "Some of the worst things in my life never happened."

Here, now, is our moment. This is our immediate, present experience and opportunity. When we stop breathing, we stop living. When we're able to train our minds, we go back to our breathing, and begin again, and again and again. Whenever you are in doubt, or even panic, first take a deep breath. I can't emphasize this enough, because when we're aware of our breath we're most alive. In this way, we're aware of whatever is actually happening in real life; we can become calmer, more centered, and less anxious, staying connected to the people in our immediate lives, no matter how noisy, confused, or hectic the situation. When we delve into the moment, we are living with all our awareness of reality. I've grown to treasure uneventful, quiet days for this reason. I'm able to savor real life as it unfolds.

Peter and I choose to live as authentically day-to-day as possible. We have the freedom to move in any direction we wish to go. We feel blessed that we have this freedom to do what we choose to do and not do what we wish not to do. This might be one of the blessings of maturity. We feel lucky. Obviously, for young parents with incessant demands on them, this Zen calm and satisfaction are more difficult to obtain, but I believe it is perfectly possible when you stay focused on right here, right now. The challenge is that this ability to stay mindful in your breath usually can't be acquired quickly or easily, and it might not be there when you most need it. I certainly wish I'd acquired this degree of mindfulness when I was younger, and I hope this crucial lesson of living in your breath will be helpful to you in all circumstances. The breath is key to finding pleasure and meaning in the moment.

There is no way to feel happy dwelling on the past or focusing on the future. Whatever phase we're in, these are the only days we have to live fully. Nostalgia for the good old days is depressing and self-defeating because they are not ours anymore. These are our real, alive, up-to-date everyday lives we're able to enjoy. They can be active, fun, and productive as we move forward in harmony with the world, living in full awareness of the moment. Savor a perfectly ripe peach. Breathe in the pristine salt air. Read a life-changing book. Visit with friends over a glass of wine. Engage in stimulating conversation. Walk the dog in nature's beauty. And, at the end of a peaceful, productive, and enjoyable day, have a good night's sleep, knowing that, fingers crossed, you can awaken and be able to repeat the ideal pleasure of every day.

This is the moment we have in the palms of our hands. It is alive with potential. How will we choose to savor it, treasure it, expand it, learn from it, and know more about the ever-expanding mysteries and revelations of the universe? If today were to be your last day on this earthly journey, how would *you* live *your* ideal day? Would you do anything differently than you are doing now? Who would you want to be with? What would you wish to do? Where would you want to be?

I try to greet each new day as though it is the first day of the rest of my life. In this frame of mind I can explore new ways to live with more balance and pleasure, see my environment with fresh eyes, engage with the wonders around me, and pay attention to my inner world with an up-to-the-moment knowledge of how I feel. The poet knows each fresh moment is bursting with opportunities. I keep reminding myself that all we have is this precious moment; we must give it our undivided attention.

Peter and I often say to each other, "This is it." This moment is what we've been waiting for; it is the culmination of all our past moments that has made this moment sublime. When we savor the moments, our lives will be well lived because one ideal moment opens our vision, giving us glimpses into the way our entire lives can and should be lived.

I know I have passed on the value of living in the moment to my daughters, and they experience my example when we are together. I feel it is a shame to merely get through situations, going through the motions. I want the process of the moment to represent me as a whole person. We should be in control of our temperaments, making our tendency an attitude of awareness as we greet each fresh opportunity. Alexandra and Brooke understand this manner of thinking and behaving in the moment. We have to continuously remind ourselves that living well takes time. It's hard to be Zen calm when you're multitasking. There is a huge difference between being busy, being fully engaged, and being overwhelmed.

There is a peculiarly characteristic human way of doing almost anything . . . all sorts of activities carried out in countless different ways. An overwhelming impression of unity emerges from this prodigious diversity of human types . . . People and societies don't submit passively to surroundings and events. People make choices based on what they want to be, to do and to become.

—René Dubos

3

Put Your Life in Good Order

Whenever I prepare for a journey I prepare as though for death.
Should I never return, all is in order. This is what life has taught me.

—*Katherine Mansfield*

Peter and I were fortunate when we eventually decided to live in Stonington permanently, because we had to completely rethink our lives. If we're going to live here full-time, how do we choose to use our spaces? How often will we go to New York City? Where will we travel now that we're no longer living in a city? Who are the best doctors in our area? Who is a good dentist? Who is a good upholsterer?

We had to find a whole team of Connecticut people to help us live the best life possible. We began by finding a lawyer, and we updated our wills. We found a family doctor whom we like. We had several false starts with landscapers, but we have everything in good shape now.

The renovation of our cottage took a year, but in this process I learned more about what I really wanted in my immediate surroundings. My favorite room in the cottage is my writing room. Not only is it completely quiet and private, but it is beautiful in its unadorned simplicity, overlooking our walled backyard garden. Blessedly, one huge window and a small one face east. As I watch the sunrise, my space becomes flooded with light.

I understand so powerfully that order precedes beauty. This small, spare space is so inspiring because first, and most important, it is mine alone. I have three favorite paintings on three walls, and Mike, our carpenter, built me a white bookcase–research cabinet. For as long as I can remember, I've been a believer that a woman should have a place she can retreat to that is hers alone. Both Alexandra and Brooke are great believers in having a room of one's own—something they know I couldn't live without.

Nothing enters this room against my will. No one but intimate family comes to say hi when I'm working. I always have fresh flowers on my old French farm desk.

The pleasure I receive every day from this sweet room would not be possible if the rest of my life was in chaos. I've learned from painful experience that if my house is a wreck, I become nervous and unfocused.

Whenever our physical surroundings are chaotic and disorganized, it is a real sign that other parts of our lives are out of balance. We all have a tendency to start out well-intentioned, and then gradually we become lazy and sloppy. There is a natural inclination for all of us to fall short of our best intentions when it comes to the beauty and organization in our rooms. Piles stack up. It's a big deal even to clean because there is so much clutter on every surface. Just like pounds on our bodies, stuff accumulates, and our eyes become tired as our rooms become trashed. People come in and out willy-nilly, make a mess, and don't clean up.

There have been many times in my life when I was so overwhelmed by the amount of unfinished work I had before me that I was in denial about my surroundings. And in family life, no matter how neat and responsible you are, there's bound to be a slob somewhere, or a child's messy friend. Being too impeccable, wanting to control everything, is a personality flaw because it makes others feel uncomfortable. But living well requires maintaining a sense of order.

I am no longer able to live in a mess. Until I have my house in good order, I am not free to put my whole life in order, and, worse, I am unable to fully live well in the moment, because I can't concentrate. When our possessions are in their right and proper places, we're free to expand our horizons, more able to tackle some other areas of our lives. When our houses are disorganized, not only does the disorder increase stress and worry but it causes procrastination in areas that are vitally important to our health and overall wellness.

Alexandra and Brooke regularly "clutter clear," go through closets to weed out what no longer fits the children and give away the things in the back that are never worn. Because they both buy in bulk to save money, they have systematic ways to store their inventories of supplies. Everything has a specific place; nothing is randomly put away. In order to keep their busy lives in order, they have strict discipline about their ever-changing storage needs.

I think I have now arrived at a place where our surroundings are truly current with our desired lifestyle, and they lay the foundation for all our other goals and plans. Our cottage now supports our practical as well as our aesthetic needs, creating an atmosphere of serene reassurance, making us receptive to taking on more serious challenges while thoroughly enjoying the process.

One of the most valuable lessons I've learned is to separate all of my household files, our checkbooks, bills, bank statements, correspondence, and anything that is not part of my writing. All of that material is stored in a walk-in closet in a downstairs study where I use the telephone, make reservations, do correspondence, and write checks. Both my writing room and the study have to be neat in order for me to function well and enjoy the activity at hand.

What I try to eliminate, as best as I can, is having slush piles of unrelated things that I'll deal with later. Far better to have an accordion file with the different categories in individual slots. I don't appreciate feeling scattered, scratching around, becoming frustrated, looking for lost documents and possessions that are out of place that are my responsibility to deal with.

We have to set up simple, efficient systems that work for particular and often quite peculiar needs. For example, if someone sends me food, I put it in the refrigerator and put a note with the sender's address on a magnet on the refrigerator door. Until I write a note of thanks, the address stays in place. And I've disciplined myself not to eat a nut or a piece of chocolate until I've written the thank-you note. Clothes to be dry-cleaned are located in the downstairs hall closet, and items to be laundered are in the bedroom closet. Laundry bags are separated in order not to have the wrong one picked up by mistake. They are also color-coded. The chartreuse and white bags are for the Laundromat; the solid-colored ones are for dry cleaning.

When I receive a book order, I don't deposit the check until I've gone to the post office to send out the book. I am as efficient as I can be in order to try to use my energy constructively and not become swamped or discouraged. When we return from a trip, I try to dig in and dig out, immediately putting the process of order in motion, anticipating settling back into the pleasure of my daily routine. Transitions initially take time, but when I accept this reality, I always feel the benefits of getting everything back in order.

Getting organized is a wonderful accomplishment. Being able to create the order, the method, and the discipline is impressive. But equally important is valuing the integrity of your system in order to have it in place for you day after day. Being sensible, we arrive at workable accommodations between our ideal arrangements and what is actually possible.

I'm absolutely certain that the care and the thoughtfulness that go into the organization of our lives lead to creativity as well as peace of mind. I want to be prepared to embrace abundant opportunities in the years ahead. We have to move intelligently through the seasons, storing out-of-season gear in appropriate, out-of-the-way spaces. Intuition helps guide you to what's important now, what makes the most sense to you.

We have to continuously reassess and reevaluate what's functioning effectively and what isn't working. Our physical spaces are meant to support all the unique requirements for us to move comfortably from one activity to another with the least amount of effort, time, and inconvenience. I'm always so happy when Alexandra or Brooke walks into the cottage and compliments me on how pretty everything looks. I smile, knowing full well how order must precede beauty.

Life is often messy. We want to be able to use our spaces and spread out. Space is room to be used, and you can feel the satisfaction of being in the flow state when your life is in good order.

All is order there, and elegance, pleasure, peace.

—Charles Baudelaire

4

Appreciate the Gift of Nature's Beauty

Nature conceals her secrets because she is sublime, not because she is a trickster.

Enough for me the mystery of the eternity of life, and the inkling of the marvellous structure of reality, together with the single-hearted endeavour to comprehend a portion, be it never so tiny, of the reason that manifests itself in nature.

—Albert Einstein

Since I was sixteen and went to New York City to study, I have lived most of my life in the city. It's been only a few years that we've lived year-round surrounded by nature's beauty. City life has its great cultural and intellectual advantages and career opportunities, but now that I've gone back to nature, I've found my greatest sense of wholeness, inner peace, and daily contentment.

I worship nature's beauty. My first memory is of being in my mother's flower garden when I was three, and the profound effect of this awakening has continued to influence my thinking about the importance of understanding nature's mysterious secrets.

I've learned that when we try to know and appreciate the laws of nature, we come to understand more about our own human nature. We come to know what's important in order to live more thoughtfully and reasonably. One of the most important things about appreciating nature is learning all there is to know about the dynamics of the world we live in, and even though we comprehend only a fragment of her secrets, we will never grow bored or tired in our curiosity and thirst to understand.

Wherever you live, as often as possible, escape into the quiet solitude of nature's power to change your mood, enlarge your perspective, increase your vision, renew your strength, give you hope, and bring you inner peace. Nature's beauty is the best antidote to our sunless technological age.

I'm pleased my daughters and grandchildren share my love of beaches. The sand, the surf, the sea air, seashells along the shore waiting to be collected, the merging spectrum of blues in the sky and water, and the sheer expansiveness of the ocean—these will always be there to restore you. Reach out to embrace the beach. Find a conch shell and listen to the sea. Display your shell collection on a tray of sand to remind you of your beach vacations. For years I had a conch shell I used as a doorstop in our New York apartment. I love seeing Alexandra's growing shell collection on a white tray table in her sunroom. Brooke and Cooper color and decorate the pebbles they find at the seashore—some of my favorite paperweights!

I feel so fortunate now to be surrounded by the seaside, beaches, islands, woods, lawns, gardens, and trees. This natural beauty all around is enormously stimulating. We have intimate access to expansive stretches of sky and clouds—the sunrises and sunsets over the harbor, the moon's first appearance as a sliver and then the lit-up sky of the full moon are enough entertainment to keep me occupied, and preoccupied, day and night. On clear evenings it's fun to sit outside and gaze up at all the wonder and mystery of the starry sky.

We never close the curtains at night because there's so much to see—the colors of the early dawn on the harbor when the sun moves from east to west are so subtle; the water shimmers like millions of diamonds undulating, dancing, and generally having a good time. We have placed our bed a foot off center in the room in order for us both to have a view of the water. Rearrange the furniture in your rooms in order to experience the best view. What is your favorite view from your windows? Alexandra and Brooke's grandmother placed her four-poster bed on an angle in her house in the Berkshires in order to see the rolling hills and trees in the early dawn. She sat up in her high bed and wrote poetry inspired by her love of nature's beauty.

Continue to use the wondrous colors from nature to refresh and uplift the rooms in your home. Use the associations from your love of beaches and gardens to bring the outside beauty in. Paint your bedroom ceiling blue to echo the sky and water. Bleach the floor to remind you of a sandy beach. If you don't have a view of nature from your window, hang a print of a garden or beach scene to expand the space and delight your eyes.

In the winter, without all the leaves on the maple trees, I have a view of Narragansett Bay as well as the ocean. Because nothing ever stands still in nature, we have a continuous feast for the eye when we're out-of-doors. In spring, we're able to experience the buds blossoming and changing color before our eyes. It's a wonderful experience to stroll in the garden at sunrise, listen to the singing birds, and hear the murmur of the bumblebees enjoying the sweet nectar from our flowers.

Wherever you are, when you walk outdoors, inhale the fresh air and look up and all around you. The ever-changing variety of nature's landscape—mountains, forests, meadows, flowers, and the ocean—will always restore you. Nature's beauty makes us feel the wonder of being a vital part of the mystery and majesty of the universe.

Because of my daughters' idea that we buy a house in order for me to have a garden, I feel the great gift now of being a country person. I've come home. I'm far more aware of all the beauty surrounding me wherever I am. Somehow, emerging into the center of nature every day opens my eyes, heart, and senses to a different form of communication. I enjoy the variety of sounds—the waves, the wind, the birds. There is a definite sense of interaction, mutuality, when I immerse myself in this extraordinary natural beauty as my regular sensuous diet.

When I first went to Bermuda, I couldn't turn my back to the beauty of the turquoise sea and the sweetness of all the flowers everywhere. Something as humble as blue morning glories climbing up whitewashed walls was strikingly beautiful to my eyes. Would I become jaded? I wondered. Would I become surfeited? Would my senses become dulled by the sheer availability of all this colorful natural beauty?

The short answer is *no*. It's not possible. I'm too passionate about nature. The more beauty I absorb, the more I seek. I was once on the telephone with Alexandra describing to her how glorious my purple irises were. I told her that as we spoke, I could see the flowers slowly opening in front of me. "You better enjoy them, Mom, because they won't last long," she said. Within a few days they had shriveled up and lost their color. When the irises are in their prime, that moment of perfection is fleeting. Everything that grows comes into being and dies: a key lesson for all of us about the nature of reality.

Even though New England has some harsh winters, thunderstorms, and hurricanes, I fully enjoy the wisdom and variety of the four seasons, the change of weather, and the flower bulbs, invisible under the snow, always appearing in the early spring. After four months of the garden in bloom, I enjoy the fall foliage that people come from all over to see. We have some roads where the trees create natural arches, and driving along these scenic streets at different times of the year is quite an experience. Seeing woods in the winter with no leaves, white birch trees, and snow with beams of sunlight streaming through the natural white columns is simply magnificent. The balance and rhythm of the four seasons is a great gift indeed.

Nature teaches us that we are not in control. We live in harmony with the rhythms of the seasons, and accept the ripening of time. We eat food that is in season and learn to respect nature's laws. When we learn to live in accord with her gifts and beauty, we are nourishing and replenishing our souls. We learn to accept the whole of nature and take a keen interest in the unique elements that cause different effects. With nature as our teacher we will be forever stimulated and challenged to accept what we have no control over. Take the seasons and weather as they come, respecting nature's power. Because we can't control nature, we learn to adapt to her powerful forces and be cautious, trying not to be in harm's way.

Our goal should be a turning toward a life of balance, harmony, order, and self-sufficiency. The serene enjoyment of a deeper knowledge and appreciation of nature will make all the difference in our lives because nature is the source of all wisdom and truth. When I meditate on her lessons, the laws of nature, and the world of living things, I feel uplifted, knowing that I'm able to appreciate her extraordinary, abundant gifts every day I'm alive.

Nature has always brought me great happiness and is available to inspire in me awe and devotion. During the happiest moments of my life and the times of my greatest pain and sorrow, the healing powers of nature's beauty have given me hope and strength to carry on. Gardens and beaches have a transforming, as well as a transporting, effect on me. The beauty is always there to move me to strong emotions, and I often turn to nature in meditation to answer my questions and teach me the lessons I need to learn about patience, acceptance, appreciation, devotion, reason, and love.

Artists, through their sensitivity to nature's inspiration, increase our awareness of beauty. Art imitates nature. If all of us ordinary people had eyes that could see the gifts of nature's beauty with great clarity and love, we wouldn't need artists. But not all people are endowed with the sensitivity, experience, passion, or talent of an artist. The artist shows us that nature loves to hint and points to miraculous beauty, color, and light.

I have a passion for the delicate beauty, color, and scent of flowers. I would only be half alive if I couldn't have flowers around me. It's not enough to see them when I'm outside; I need them to feed my soul in the rooms where I spend time. A lesson I've learned is to always have fresh flowers at home, and I'm pleased that my daughters have carried on this tradition. Both Alexandra and Brooke value the positive energy that flowers bring to their rooms, and they have flowers or flowering plants indoors year-round.

Flowers bring nature's beauty into our spaces and expand our souls, increasing our joy and pleasure. I love arranging flowers, and tending them is so relaxing to me. Flowers speak to us in a silent meditation about the sacredness of being alive, and the power of their beauty calls forth our emotions. Flowers are from creation. Why is the wonder of flowers such an inspiring, important part of nature? What is the reason we have flowers if not to increase our appreciation for life? Always make it a priority to have fresh flowers and flowering plants at home. They have the power to reduce stress and boost your mood. Before you take a trip, put a vase of flowers in fresh water in the refrigerator at home so they will greet you upon your return.

Nature's beauty is what sustains us, guides us, speaks to us, and inspires our higher levels of conscious awareness and intuition. There is more light on our paths when we dedicate ourselves to spending more time observing and contemplating nature's gifts. This choice will fill the rest of our lives with both knowledge and understanding as we patiently tend to the silent wisdom of our roses.

Whenever you have the opportunity, retreat into nature to refresh your spirit. A twenty-minute stroll in a park or on a pretty, tree-lined street will increase your mental skills. Living in the country allows me to boost my energy, and regularly going for walks and exposing myself to sunlight and nature's beauty has made all the difference in the quality of my life. This quiet gift nourishes every aspect of my being as my reverence for nature increases by the hour with my praise. I want you to experience this same delight and inspiration. I'm forever grateful that Alexandra and Brooke share with me the wisdom of the gift of nature's beauty.

Slowly I discovered the secret of my art. It consists of a meditation on nature, on the expression of a dream which is always inspired by reality.

—*Henri Matisse*

5

....

Waste Not

To waste, to destroy, our natural resources, to skin and exhaust the land instead of using it so as to increase its usefulness, will result in undermining in the days of our children the very prosperity which we ought by right to hand down to them amplified and developed.

—Theodore Roosevelt

Many of us were raised with the proverb "Waste not, want not." I hate to waste any precious resource. When I see others thoughtlessly wasting, it hurts my feelings. I want to be part of the solution of preserving our fragile planet Earth, not part of its destruction. Our surroundings and the environment we live in are sacred, and humanity, through industry, is destroying our planet, making us sick, and killing us.

The book *Silent Spring*, by U.S. naturalist and writer Rachel Carson, woke me up. Carson wrote, "Over increasingly large areas of the United States, spring now comes unheralded by the return of the birds, and the early mornings are strangely silent when once they were filled with the beauty of bird song." What a chilling thought. And then I read on and realized it isn't just the beauty of birds but the beauty of children and innocent people who are continuously exposed to chemical toxins in pesticides that are mysteriously making us sick to death.

Pregnant women who are exposed to harmful pesticides are highly likely to have babies with low IQs, and there is a strong possibility that these children will have developmental problems. The real catch-22 is that these toxic chemicals are brought home from the supermarket, and unless fruits and vegetables are rinsed thoroughly, the expecting mother will poison herself and her in-the-womb baby. What we don't know *can* hurt us. I find this rather frightening.

Look for the cause in every effect. What about global warming or the poisons in the air from power plants and aerosols? There's more here than meets the eye. If an ounce of prevention is worth a pound of cure, how can we be too careful? Chemical pesticides and fertilizers and radiation are silent killers. This is as serious as things get, and in order for us to survive, we have an obligation to know. One can, through social actions, make a difference. Vote intelligently and stay as informed as possible. The balance of dangers from nuclear power as opposed to coal power plants is part of an ongoing discussion that will affect our grandchildren.

On and off different parts of the country have had serious water shortages, where restaurants didn't serve water unless a customer asked for it. I remember being in New York City during several blackouts and how dreadful it was for our apartment building not to have running water. I am married to a wonderful man, and I've found Peter reasonable about most things, but when it comes to his water consumption, he is recklessly irresponsible, and I have made it one of my causes to try to reform him. He loves water. He's a Pisces, the twelfth sign of the zodiac. He's basically a *fish*. He closes the bathroom door and runs hot water full blast for the entire time he likes to spend leisurely shaving. Then, he switches the heavy gush from hot to cold, waiting for it to get nice and icy before he methodically brushes his teeth.

He's been oblivious to this thoughtless waste of pure water, which could become as valuable as oil in the future. I inquired among friends how they try to conserve water, and I received a range of interesting answers. One friend shaves in the shower to save water, because, he told me, the higher your water bill, the higher your sewer bill. Another friend sets a kitchen timer for only five minutes and then immediately turns off the water when the timer goes off. Peter and I save water by showering together. Some people don't flush their toilets at night to conserve water.

Peter has finally caught on that it irritates me when he needlessly wastes water. He's slowly come to realize that when I cheerfully remind him, "Watch the water," I mean, "Turn off the water." I use only the glass express cycle on the dishwasher in order to save water. Any kind of waste is a waste.

I want to live well but not extravagantly. I don't have a car, because I don't need a car, and I don't really like to drive. I'm grateful to the people who cheerfully drive me and Peter where we want to go. I realize the amount of gas used to move us about is the same whether it is in my car or someone else's; however, the less we use a car, the better for everyone. Whether you're driving or being driven, do it as little as possible. We often walk about the village and don't get into a car for weeks on end.

I loathe wasting food, too. I have a really bad habit of eating everything on my plate, a remnant from my childhood days of the Clean Plate Club. Sometimes there is too much food and I eat too much to prevent the waste of throwing it out. Portion control is key to this situation. We have friends who, whenever they eat out, each order a sandwich, eat half, and take the rest home. Why waste? I inquired about the logic. "Why not order one sandwich and share it?" Dave is the cook in their house, and he smiled and said, "I'm a leftover guy." He loves to have all the fixings he can use at home for another meal. The leftover food people take home from restaurants is not necessarily for their dogs. By saving it, they are conserving energy while saving time and money.

What are some of the areas where you are reducing your environmental footprint? Some people go around their houses and turn off lights. Others have switched to more energy-efficient lightbulbs. I cut up all the unwritten-on paper from the pads I write on to use for jotting notes. Peter and I wear our clothes until they're worn out. Some people reuse water bottles. I use old newspapers as packing materials. I save and reuse gift wrapping.

I have evolved into much more of a conservationist. I have become more conscientious about recycling, and I learned from Alexandra to always return plastic keys to the hotel desks so they can be reprogrammed, rather than have the plastic end up taking a million years to disappear. I try to use as little plastic as possible. For example, I never use Styrofoam cups. Alexandra's children use colorful, washable cloth pouches for their snacks rather than Ziploc bags. New Orleans doesn't recycle, so when Alexandra goes to visit her best friend there, she brings her friend's newspapers and empty water bottles back home to Maryland to recycle.

Clearly, there are small things we can all do to avoid waste. In a post office in Maryland, I was waiting in line to be served and saw a rack of recycled shopping bags printed with the words:

USA GO GREEN

BUY LOCAL PRODUCE

REUSE BAGS

CHOOSE TO WALK

GO GREEN—REDUCE OUR ENVIRONMENTAL FOOTPRINT USA

RIDE A BIKE

RECYCLE MORE

Go green. Reduce. Reuse. Recycle. I bought these tote bags for the grands. They loved them and thought I was "cool."

I'm glad to observe how careful our grandchildren are about not wasting precious resources. They are extremely conscientious about waste, saving wherever they can. Alexandra even recycles toilet paper rolls. Her family's dog poop bags are 100 percent biodegradable, and she sent a bunch of these earth-friendly bags to me for our recycling. Her children don't use plastic to floss their teeth.

Any kind of waste is thoughtless. Whether we waste our potential talents, our own time, our limited resources, our money, or other people's time, each of us can become more aware and conscientious. The smallest good habits accumulate to an enormous contribution toward making a difference. It's a good feeling to know in our hearts we are doing our best in a world that is in serious trouble. By focusing on saving fossil fuel, oil, water, paper, food, and clothing, we will be doing our part to cut down on waste.

None of us can completely avoid hazardous waste or the carcinogenic agents in our lives. A few miles down the road from our cottage we have a nuclear power plant. But there are clearly more questions we should be asking and more independent scientific research conducted about these environmentally perilous situations that put us all at risk.

We must keep reminding ourselves that it is easier to get into something than it is to get out of it. This vast desecration of our land is fairly recent in the history of our evolution. We have the power to stop being wasteful so that our grandchildren's children will be able to flourish, and to hear the cheerful sound of birds announcing the arrival of spring. We can't solve all the problems of waste, but we can encourage mindfulness.

Waste not!

Man has been endowed with reason and creative powers to increase what has been given him, but so far he has not created but destroyed. There are fewer and fewer forests, the rivers are drying up, the game birds are becoming extinct, the climate is ruined, and every day the earth is becoming poorer and more hideous.

—Anton Chekhov

6

Don't Do What You Don't
Want to Do—Delegate!

We only do well the things we like doing.

—Colette

Brooke and I were both working in the downstairs study that faces the garden and harbor. Cooper was having a nap, and the cottage was sweetly quiet—a moment's peace. As I gazed out the window in a mood of satisfaction and pleasure, I saw our landscape gardener arrive with a helper. I felt a great sense of relief that I didn't have to lose my focus and deadhead the geraniums or prune the roses after they'd lost their last bloom.

I actually like pruning the rosebushes, and when I'm in the mood to set aside the time, I get in a meditative trance and thoroughly enjoy the experience. But when we've had a storm and the garden looks pathetically neglected, I have too much pride to overlook things. Often, against my better judgment, I prune out of necessity rather than desire, and, because the roses are on the street side of the house, tourists and friends who stop to chat can make this process quite lengthy.

Isn't it wonderful to be able to call on experts who know and love what they're doing to free us up to do what we're good at, allowing us to carry on with our chosen, scheduled commitments?

I'm finally realistic about the fact that there is only so much time, and I intend to continue to be highly selective about how I spend it and how I use my energy. Often, as a reward for having devoted my time to working, I'll go into the garden, clippers in hand, and putter, bringing some flowers inside to arrange, but without any pressure. I'm fortunate to be able to afford help with the yard work and realize how blessed I am. We all have to choose what we do ourselves and what we'll pay others to do for us.

It is exceedingly useful to understand the benefits of paying others to do tasks they can do well and often more efficiently than we can. We should try to spend our time, as much as is practical, doing things only we can do, and these are different for each of us and often highly specific. Often when I ask Alexandra or Brooke if there is something I can do to help them, they'd love to say yes, but there's an ever-increasing number of things they can't delegate, as is the case for most of us. Only you can write a sympathy note to a friend or go see someone in the hospital, or watch your child's basketball game. But there are many things we *can* delegate, giving us time to do other things that will enormously enrich our lives.

I have learned the beauty of delegation from my daughters, who are smart about the ways they appropriately delegate and who make thoughtful suggestions about how I can have others help me. I emphasize choice. Some people have to make hard choices because of their financial situations. However, it is often worthwhile to hire someone to do something that you want done or that needs to be done rather than doing it yourself, even if the costs are high.

When we delegate, however, we have to be meticulous about the people we hire. I use my instincts, as well as my desire to give money to people I like, people I admire for their expertise, people I enjoy being with. Unfortunately, no matter where you live, there are people of bad character who look for ways to take advantage of others. What I've learned is to delegate, but not too much, and to trust the people who help us, and then cross my fingers.

I don't look for trouble, but when it is obvious, I try to take care of the problem immediately. It's wise to avoid being under contract, so that if you switch to another company there are no complications. Even if the people who serve you are honest, they may be too expensive or too casual, not respectful of your time. We are in tight economic times, and there are plenty of hard workers who would love the opportunity to work for you. If you're having a lawn party and the grass was scheduled to be mowed beforehand but the crew didn't show up, this is an unnecessary irritation. When I delegate, I expect the people I hire to be reliable and give me their best work. One of the benefits of having others help us is to get things done on time and well, with the least amount of frustration.

Last August, Alexandra and her family went for their annual beach vacation in North Carolina. The house they rented is pet friendly, so they were able to bring their beloved Homer and save the expense of their dog sitter. When Alexandra called us saying she had good news, I sat down, looked out at the garden, and said, "Bring it on. Nothing pleases me more than good news." She knew that what she was going to tell me would thrill me. "Mom, I've hired a woman to help out while we're on vacation. She can look after Homer when we're at the beach, and wash and cut up fruit, husk corn, and do the laundry. I figured out that it will be the same cost as I would have paid for a dog sitter and we get to be with Homer."

Typically, family vacations are exhausting for the mother, who understands all the quirky needs of her family and ends up being a slave to the endless tasks that have to be done for things to run smoothly. I was so happy to hear Alexandra's news, my whole body tingled with relief for her. She has such a high-pressure job that she oftentimes feels it is unsustainable. No one deserves a vacation more than Alexandra, and because she was smart enough to delegate, she had a relaxing, fun time with her family and came home refreshed after her break.

I had someone help me clean our cottage, but she abandoned me abruptly to go work at a casino in Las Vegas. That proved to be a blessing. Because I paid her by the hour, she did less and less in more and more time. I now have a cleaning service where a husband and wife come—on schedule. They bring their own supplies and they tear through the house. They're instructed not to touch anything in our writing rooms except to vacuum the floors, so there is no interruption to our work. They're in and out, and the place gleams and smells like a sea breeze. I couldn't be more pleased.

Plato taught that "more will be accomplished, and better, and with more ease, if every man does what he is better fitted to do, and nothing else." Choose what you want to do, what you're able to do without feeling burdened. If you find yourself complaining, it's probably a sign you need more help from others.

I feel richly supported by everyone who works for us and am deeply grateful for the many generous acts of kindness they shower on us throughout the year. Bob, our contractor, watches the cottage when we're away. Mike, our carpenter, loves his work. He says, "Give me some wood and I'll make something." He gives us white hydrangeas from his garden every August, and his wife bakes cookies for us at Christmastime. When Debbie delivers the laundry, she drives us to the post office or to our favorite seaside restaurant if the weather is too stormy for us to walk.

When we leave the village, Brooke encourages us to have our suitcases shipped from New York City to our cottage via United Parcel Service in order to have an easier train ride home. We ship our dirty clothes home from Maryland when we visit Alexandra rather than dragging them to New York, where we spend a night or two before going home to Stonington. Whenever we intelligently entrust something to others that will lighten our load or help us live better, it is valuable and worth the money.

Last winter we hired a college student to drive Peter and me around. Darcy lives across the street and is the daughter of our dear friends Mary Ellen and Rick. It was pleasant for us to spend some time with her and to discover how reliable, smart, and fun she is to be with—a young lady we enjoyed watching grow up.

When we're at a restaurant and a sudden storm causes us to need a ride home, rather than hiring a taxi to pick us up, we have one of the waiters drive us. We always give him or her a sweetener for "the fund"—the college fund.

Many hands do noble, good work, and I'm appreciative of all the resources we have that support our needs. Nothing we do should ever be done reluctantly, because reluctance makes something easy into something difficult. It is the law of nature to give what we can and help one another where we can. When we do a job right and gladly, we are doing dignified work we can be proud of. Never let anything become drudgery, because doing so will cost you too much in negative energy. Let people who will love the work help you, and be glad they can provide for their families. As we all know, all honest work is dignified. There is a sense of victory in doing something well.

I've worked hard all of my life and don't feel guilty accepting paid help. As a friend likes to point out to me, "Just because you can, doesn't mean you should." So true. I have a great deal of energy and I'm capable of doing a lot of different things, and saving money where we can is a responsible goal. At the same time, I'm earning money and feel it is my responsibility to choose how to spend it, as I choose how to spend my time. I don't think it is appropriate for me to risk pulling my back out scrubbing the kitchen floor or get on a ladder to change a recessed lightbulb in the ceiling, risking a fall.

There are plenty of little, quick things I enjoy doing around the house, but I'm not looking for more work, I'm looking for relief. I accept all the help I can get. Now that I'm in the swing of delegating, my life seems to be running smoothly, on an even keel, thanks to all the skilled people who make this accomplishment possible. Every little bit helps the engine run.

"We only do well," St. Thomas Aquinas knew, "which is done with joy." I'll always make time to iron Cooper's dresses, my cotton clothes, or a shirt for Peter. Most of Peter's shirts are done by the dry cleaners, but there are some pastel striped and checked ones I adore ironing as I look out through our bedroom to the harbor, giving me a chance to muse about my work and my life. Ironing, for me, is a labor of love and helps me clear my head. And because I love to iron, I'm quite good at it! Most of the work I do takes a long time to show any results. When I iron I see results within minutes, and this is encouraging. But, even though I enjoy ironing, I don't overdo it, because then it wouldn't be fun.

It is worthwhile making financial sacrifices in order to do more of the things you love to do, in order to spend more time enjoying your children and your spouse. When Alexandra and Brooke were growing up, I paid someone to do laundry, tidy up the apartment, and prepare supper in order for me to spend time having fun with my daughters. Time is sacred; money is a tool.

There are two words I wish to say to all the people who help Peter and me, and my daughters' families: thank you.

Success follows doing what you want to do.
There is no other way to be successful.

—Malcolm Forbes

7

....

Avoid Unnecessary Distractions

Only those who know the supremacy of the intellectual life . . . can understand the grief of one who falls from that serene activity into the absorbing soul-wasting struggle with worldly annoyances.

—George Eliot

In *Things I Want My Daughters to Know*, I wrote about the "Five-Hour Rule." Try never to be with someone for more than five hours at a stretch. Give the other person a break!

Here I want to discuss the one-hour rule. In 1968, when I started writing, I made a pact with myself that no matter where I am or what is happening in my life, I faithfully spend one hour alone every day and fiercely protect my privacy. Everyone should be able to find a minimum of sixty minutes a day, in one continuous stretch, for their own use.

This time alone without distractions—when you're free to get away from others, to do whatever the spirit moves you to do, to think your own thoughts, to read or study or write—will become absolutely indispensable to you. I would be an imbalanced person without this private commitment to myself. If a harried writer takes that one hour, seven days a week, at the same time each day, he will in all probability have a book by the end of the year.

All great people who have made major contributions to society, throughout history, in a vast range of disciplines, have valued their solitude and needed it in order to develop their talents and perfect their craft. And one hour a day is only a small fraction of what geniuses require to do their serious work. For us to be effective in our chosen work, we have to fiercely guard against interruptions and be free, alone, to concentrate for expansive blocks of time. If you know that you are going into a silent room every day at the same time, your subconscious does wonders. Two hours would be even better, but I realize that many people, particularly the young, can't afford it.

For purity of thinking, to work through difficult mental challenges, it is essential to be undisturbed. The one-hour rule is vital. Distractions make you feel scattered and discouraged. Whenever we become sidetracked and diverted, we become frustrated. Of course there will be interruptions. There always have been, and people will break in on us and we will lose our train of thought. But these times should be the exception, not the rule, if we are to be able to live lives of meaning and purpose. Our attention becomes fractured by the thousand and one details and interruptions in everyday life.

Who among us is so strongly disciplined as to be able to say that nothing ever interferes with our ability to concentrate? When we put ourselves in a position where we are alone and quiet and able to direct our thoughts and focus our energy, great satisfaction results. And when we dilute our attention, we become nervous and anxious because we feel guilty that we are wasting our precious time, keeping ourselves from what really brings us a sense of fulfillment and pleasure.

Of course there will be good days, when it is easy to get in the flow state, and there will be days when our minds are cluttered with doubts and fears. But, in this all-too-short life span, it is such a waste to live superficially. By committing to the one-hour rule, you are showing up and being receptive to the precious sixty uninterrupted minutes a day that can accumulate into significance and increase your satisfaction over the years.

Because of our ability to instantly distract ourselves through technology, we can easily lose our inner-directedness and become outer-directed. There is only so much time, energy, and money. Our first responsibilities are to take care of ourselves and our families, to accomplish our work in the best ways we can, and to have some precious face-to-face time for people we know and care about. It shouldn't be quaint that we want to meet for a visit over coffee.

In order to regain control over your life, I believe that you can schedule certain times when you are online and certain times when you are offline. For instance, you can leave your technology downstairs while you are upstairs. It's important to not always be available to others, and I admire that Alexandra and Brooke have times when they choose to disconnect, deciding not to check their e-mail, out of respect for the people they're with. Brooke doesn't answer her cell phone when she is having quality time with Cooper, and both my daughters unplug at mealtimes. This is an important lesson for all of us to honor.

There are sacred times when being unplugged is intelligent and shows respect and love for others. Because Peter and I feel uncomfortable around technology, we find it not only distracting but particularly irritating when we're with others who continuously check their e-mail. Better to excuse yourself from the table as if you are going to the bathroom than to be insensitive, especially when you know how unsettling it is to people who are not plugged in 24/7.

Many of you get up early in order to exercise. Physical exercise is essential, and somehow we have to find ways to work that into our schedule, but we shouldn't choose to take better care of our physiological needs at the expense of setting our minds on fire. We need to be fit, in mind *and* body.

If you've established the one-hour rule for your mind, looking forward to that hour is a way to feel less anxious. A combination of physical and mental exercise might give you the best possible benefits you are seeking. If you discover that you are more mentally alert in the early morning, you can switch your exercise routine to the evening in order to have the one-hour rule be most productive.

Keep in mind that being one click away is both good news and bad news. No human being can or should be available all the time. I've found that the more we are available, the greater the tendency for others to take advantage of our time. We can establish strict rules and adhere to them. No normal, creative person can or should always be tethered to her cordless gadgets. It's all right to blur the line between work and life as long as you give your own passionate interests uninterrupted blocks of time and don't devote everything to others' endless demands. When Alexandra and Brooke were toddlers, I found it most practical for me to get up at five o'clock because they slept until seven. Between five and seven I was assured time to myself without being disturbed.

By declaring that we will spend one hour a day alone, we will be paying regular attention to our basic needs. We need to isolate ourselves as part of the rhythm of a twenty-four-hour day in order to learn more about our unique needs and to remove ourselves from the pressures we all face. Some of you will meditate, others will choose to write in a journal, others will paint. The key is the consistency of time of day. What you do with the time, of course, will vary depending on your goals.

You can't achieve this deep sense of fulfillment unless you value your right to avoid unnecessary distractions by adopting the one-hour rule in order to engage in your own chosen work.

I set a kitchen timer. Alexandra gave me a color-changing one that is all white at sixty minutes and becomes pink, showing how quickly time flies by. The tick-tock keeps me company until the timer is all pink and the alarm goes off. After it rings, I can reset it for another hour if time permits.

Making a firm date with yourself and keeping it will put you in high spirits. Daniel Goleman wrote, "Good moods, while they last, enhance the ability to think flexibly and with more complexity, thus making it easier to find solutions to problems, whether intellectual or interpersonal." There is nothing as richly satisfying as keeping your agreement with yourself. The more you do, the better your mood. In the forty-five years since Alexandra was born, I've faithfully logged in two hours a day—that adds up to 33,114 hours, including eleven leap years! People who can afford only one hour a day would have accumulated 16,689 hours in forty-five years. Think of the accomplishments you will accrue and the benefits you will score when you have this consistency of focus.

Our character discipline is key. If we allow endless distractions to interrupt us, chaos will follow and we will become weary. Success in anything comes through consistency of focus. When we give our complete attention to something, there is total inner silence. We will interrupt ourselves—we always do—yet we have no one else to blame. No one has the power over you to obstruct your progress. As Gertrude Stein understood, "I like a view but I like to sit with my back turned to it." Don't hinder yourself!

Try to concentrate your powers toward your own goals. Be tenacious. Persevere. Remain focused and persistent. Mental discipline is a great and lasting moral virtue. Don't be a saboteur and break this vitally important rule. Regular, uninterrupted concentration gives you the opportunity to live up to your potential as you make this one-hour rule a discipline you look forward to every day, with no exceptions. You will be contemplating life using your highest intelligence.

The person who practices this exercise of concentration sees the universe with new eyes, as if he were seeing it for the first and the last time.

In his enjoyment of the present, he discovers the splendor and mystery of existence and of the world's emergence; at the same time, he achieves serenity by experiencing how relative are the things which provoke anxiety and worry.

—Pierre Hadot

8

....

Surround Yourself with Stimulating People

My essential pattern is suited to communication and revelation. I am all in the open and in full view, born for company and friendship.

—*Michel de Montaigne*

I think of myself as a student, eager to learn from being in the company of accomplished people who are wiser and more excellent than I am and who set a high standard by their own examples. It's inspiring to know that some of their knowledge has the power to transform us from being narrow-minded to thinking more universally.

Of course, the more we learn, the more we discover how little we know, and it is crucially important to our own intellectual stimulation to be highly selective not only about the people we surround ourselves with but also about what we read. When we have a hunger for learning, we can expand our stimulation by being in the company of great minds.

Montaigne believed that learned people can help us to become learned, but that we alone become wise by our own wisdom. I love to believe that I'm able to think for myself, and I do, with a great deal of help from brilliant minds.

The exceptionally bright people I've been fortunate to have in my life have encouraged me, and have helped me to realize that we all can be roused to greater activity and heightened action. I want people to excite me and set a good example for me to model, even if my contributions are a small drop in the ocean of life.

We have a huge classroom, the entire universe, and we have ancient philosophers who can excite us in our everyday lives. Think of the style of Socrates' teachings in Plutarch's words:

> Socrates did not set up grandstands for his audience and did not sit upon a professorial chair; he had no fixed timetable for talking or walking with his friends. Rather, he did philosophy sometimes by joking with them, or by drinking or going to war or to the market with them, and finally by going to prison and drinking poison.
> He was the first to show that at all times and in every place, in everything that happens to us, daily life gives us the opportunity to do philosophy.

We need to exercise our minds with constant nourishment just as we sustain our bodies with nutritious food. I had a wonderful exercise teacher in New York City who was a professional dancer; she was so stimulating to be around, and she made her class practically jump for joy. She'd clap her hands and click her heels and sing to the music. Some of the older women in her class were a bit uptight and, to put it kindly, rigid, but after an hour running around a church basement gym, even they loosened up and got into the free, spontaneous flow of movement. Liz would be in the center of the space, with us all in a wide circle, and she'd move in joyous gestures of playfulness. "Don't suck off my energy. Come on; get your own energy going."

If we are realistic, we'll reason with ourselves that stimulating people want us to be stimulating also. We, too, can be the positive spirit-energy to others and share our own sparks of passion. We can strive to become as stimulating as the bright company we enjoy being with. When we think of all the people who give us the most pleasure, we realize that they have a twinkle in their eye, they make us think, they make us question things from every possible point of view, they teach us about ourselves, and they make us laugh. The people who bring light to our lives become our torchbearers, leading the way, helping us with some illumination on the long, dark path toward being educated and, in time, enlightened.

It's natural to be attached to people who have achieved excellence, who are dedicated to what they're doing, who tell interesting stories, who suggest books for us to read, who introduce us to their friends, and who take an interest in our lives. We try to emulate them, and if we're fortunate enough to develop friendships with them over time, these rare and fascinating souls will also learn from us, from our different perspectives. It is thrilling to have this interchange of different points of view.

The stimulant of good conversation is the greatest addiction. Nikos Kazantzakis, the author of *Zorba the Greek*, urges us to never be satisfied, but to "be always restless, unsatisfied, unconforming."

Zorba teaches us to keep alert. Not all vital and stimulating people are great philosophers or writers. Many exciting people come in disguise. There's wisdom in the old man and the sea. These stimulating people inspire us to undertake heightened activity, to keep climbing toward the radiant light of ultimate truth and the profound wisdom of reason. These giant souls show us the big view of life's miraculous gifts always available to us.

In 1989, when I was writing *Living Beautifully Together*, my editor was critical of me for beginning my chapter on friends claiming that I'd rather be with Alexandra and Brooke than with anyone else in the world. I'm humbled to say that I have consistently felt this way throughout their development, over so many years. Now that they are middle-aged and have children of their own, not only are my daughters the most stimulating people in my life but I find my grandchildren equally exciting and fun to be with—age apparently doesn't matter! I'll never forget Alexandra teasing me when she was a teenager, telling me that unless I was fun to be with, she and Brooke could ditch me. A family expression is that they could give me "a wide berth."

My daughters stir me up, excite me, and inspire me to live the best life possible. I value their approval and thrive on their love. This book is a love story to my daughters, and I believe this dedication is genuine and honest. The truth is the prize. I realize that to be a devoted mother to my grown daughters is to be in a dream relationship, and, while I can't speak for them, I believe the bond is reciprocal. I've invested so much of myself in this mother-daughter sharing; I feel we are on such solid ground that we can be ready for the surprises and challenges ahead.

Even when I'm being self-congratulatory, in a playful way, Brooke will laugh and say, "There's only one sweet Mom."

My desire is to continue to be stimulating to Alexandra, Brooke, and my grandchildren in the exciting years of adventure and discovery ahead.

Judgment can be acquired only by acute observation, by actual experience in the school of life, by ceaseless alertness to learn from others, by study of the activities of men who have made noble marks, by striving to analyze the everyday play of causes and effects, by constant study of human nature.

—B. C. Forbes

9

Be Prepared for Disappointments

Everything in life that we really accept undergoes a change.
So suffering must become love. That is the mystery.

—Katherine Mansfield

When we learn how to deal with disappointments, we avoid pain and suffering.

When Peter and I were in New York last spring, we had a breakfast with Brooke where we learned that we had a last-minute opportunity to go to Paris with Brooke and Cooper because Brooke's husband, Tony, was going there on business. It was almost too good to be true; their hotel bill would have been Tony's company expense and we could all chip in with our airline miles. The thought of Peter and his youngest grandchild, Cooper, in Paris together was a dream come true. The stars were all aligned.

Brooke was to call us only if I was needed on the telephone to speak with an agent about transferring the frequent-flier miles. We were giddily happy. A few hours later, while Peter and I were having lunch,

Brooke called, and I ran out of the restaurant in order to take the call. She told me that Tony's business trip was canceled. "What? Is it just postponed?" I couldn't believe my ears.

"Mom, not postponed. Canceled."

It took me a few minutes to regain my composure. Peter and I had become attached to this prospect, and all signals had seemed to be go. Still in shock, I broke the bad news to my husband. "What a shame," he said. "That's really too bad. I was really looking forward to this." Peter looked at me with a sad face and inquired, "Why? What happened?" Brooke didn't have details, and had been so disappointed she hadn't wanted to talk long—she had actually been in a meeting when she got the bad news.

I felt Peter's pain and saw it in my husband's face. "How do you deal with disappointment?" I asked him.

He looked deep into my eyes and paused. "Badly!"

We had a good laugh, and our food arrived at the table. We didn't lose our appetite over the news, and the reality was that we were off to Paris, alone, to celebrate our thirty-seventh anniversary the next day. The family trip to Paris would have been a month later, not exactly spread out evenly, and the practical side of us reasoned that it just wasn't meant to be.

Of course, there are far deeper disappointments in life. I remember when I had a miscarriage before I became pregnant with Alexandra, my way of working through my pain was not to talk about it. I chose to keep it to myself because I don't like when people feel sorry for me. It fuels the pain. I went to a fertility specialist because I feared I wouldn't be able to give birth to a healthy baby. My doctor was reassuring, and soon I became pregnant with Alexandra.

Another time I was deeply disappointed was when my publisher turned down my book about happiness. I cried and then went back to my writing room to work. I can be disappointed about a lot of things, but when there is something I can do to improve a situation, I try my best. My publisher and editor took me to lunch and asked me what makes *me* happy. The pain of rejection suddenly had been transformed into a new direction—how to write about this elusive subject. I was now inspired to write a more deeply personal, intimate book about happiness.

The way to approach disappointment has not been better expressed than in theologian Reinhold Niebuhr's Serenity Prayer.

> God, grant us grace
> to accept with serenity
> the things that cannot be changed,
> courage to change the things
> that should be changed,
> and the wisdom to distinguish
> the one from the other.

The most important lesson in life is to accept and be at peace with what we have no power to change. I'm in favor of hoping for the best possible outcome in all situations, but I'm no stranger to disappointments, and, so far, I have survived the storms that fate has put in my immediate path. We have to be in good shape, with strength of character and indomitable determination, in order to face the hardships that will be inevitable to us in the future years.

Human beings are highly capable of adapting to situations that they aren't able to alter. The French writer and philosopher Simone de Beauvoir knew that "in the face of an obstacle which is impossible to overcome, stubbornness is stupid." Not only should we look for ways to adapt and be flexible but we have to make compromises and changes to best accommodate what happens to us.

"Be prepared," the Girl Scout motto, is good advice, and, when we are prepared, we find life more enjoyable, day to day. Whether we prepare a meal or a lecture, we have to have everything we need at hand in order to have the best possible outcome. If you've ever tried to follow a recipe and then realized you're missing one ingredient, you remember the frustration of having to run to the store to buy whatever you forgot.

We can prepare for a vacation, but we can't control everything about our experience. We need to equip ourselves with a toolbox of virtues in order to accept what is not in our power to change. Understanding what is in your control and what isn't is key to managing your expectations. Many things in our lives are disappointing and far from our expectations, desires, and hopes, but we can't revert to doom and gloom without making ourselves and everyone around us miserable. Often we make ourselves unhappy because we have unreasonable expectations about outcomes. As William Makepeace Thackeray reminds us, "Bravery never goes out of fashion."

I, personally, don't prepare myself for all the unimaginable possibilities and unknown events that could take place. None of us has a clue; strange things happen. Rather than wasting my energy worrying about what might or might not happen, I try to remain focused on the things I can do now that might bring positive results in the future. Rather than attempting to predict the unknown, I prefer to hold the assumption that everything is going to work out, and when my efforts are thwarted and I become frustrated, I go back to the drawing board and take a deep breath, feeling a deeper sense of commitment and passion for what I believe to be important. Take disappointments as challenges.

How can we hold fast to our highest ideals and not become discouraged by the seemingly insurmountable global problems? If you can be part of a resolution, move toward that goal. If you can't, continue to work on areas of your life you have the power to improve. I know that a lot of our problems we bring on ourselves because we don't want to confront reality. There is a tendency to point a finger at someone we can blame or to feel sad when a happy time is over. Denial is a defense mechanism we use to refuse to acknowledge painful realities, thoughts, or feelings. Nothing, good or bad, is permanent. We become frustrated when we don't accept impermanence, even though rationally we understand nothing is lasting; everything passes with time.

We always seem to want to bottle everything that is good. We don't want our baby to grow up, and we don't want to grow old. When things are going well, we don't want anything to change, although we rationally know that everything that lives is in continuous transformation. Cute babies become interesting children and then adults. One of the best ways to prepare yourself for disappointments that are impossible to avoid or prevent is to completely absorb yourself in all the good in each moment.

I like to think of problems as situations, and pain as an inevitable part of life. It is normal to seek pleasure and try to avoid pain. We should continue to want pleasure in our daily lives, but we must be realistic about the certainty of pain. Just as it is natural to want to feel happy and not sad, we all know that sometimes we can't help feeling sorrowful because of the circumstances.

As we've learned from experience, things could always be a whole lot worse. Life will demand strength from us. We have to fight back and not give in. Words of wisdom from someone who nobly served in Iraq: "Soldier on." The rough patches we survive teach us how to strengthen our inner resources. We should make the best of things in our control and carry on.

Don't look for trouble. That's bad luck. But when situations knock at the door, meet them head-on, knowing you didn't ask for this and you'll do everything in your power to act appropriately and not turn your back. Don't pretend everything is okay when it is not. Wouldn't we like to be able to say, "I don't want to deal with this"? But we know we must play with the hand we've been dealt and move on. Be patient, be kind, and, above all, be a good sport. We have to learn to be flexible when conditions that are beyond our control change, and adapt by making adjustments after we know the facts. One thing always does lead to another.

We can't carry the weight of the world's problems on our shoulders without becoming depressed. Life goes on. We will face adversity, but we will meet our challenges far better when we look for the bright spots and focus on the things that bring us joy and hope. Being aware of agonizing situations doesn't mean we want to dwell on them. If we constantly think about the problems all over the world and in our personal lives, we'll become discouraged. There are plenty of storms wherever we look, but it is healthier to focus on specific things we can do to help, and enjoy all the enormous good in our immediate lives.

Be not afraid. Be resilient. All of us are subject to the agonies and ecstasies of life. We have strength inside us, at our core, that we've never had to use, but it is there, just in case. Let's all strive to be well adjusted. Don't feel unique in your painful challenges; everyone has their own emotionally difficult burdens to bear. The best defense against being let down by things beyond our control is to have our emotional tools in working order, greased and sharp, ready for us to press them into use.

We can't control nature or human nature, but we can control our attitudes and how we react. Things will always come and go, and there will be surprises, good and bad. We can accept and adjust to the changes, and become mindful of everything that happens. And, in this exciting journey, we can learn to never take anything for granted; as we become stronger and more understanding, our disappointments will take a backseat in our lives.

I greatly admire the way Alexandra and Brooke handle their own disappointments. They have been raised to eagerly anticipate events, but also to keep their expectations low enough to enjoy the satisfactions of day-to-day reality. Even when faced with sudden, unexpected situations, my daughters will say, "I'm fine," or "I don't want to be sad when I'm happy," and then they tell me the disappointing news—sometimes unspeakably sad. They never feel sorry for themselves. None of us are in the habit of complaining about the little discouraging things that we all encounter in our daily lives, but when it comes to serious situations, both of my daughters and I tend to be strong.

Most of my disappointments have been in the world of publishing. Alexandra always reminds me to think back when everything turned out so beautifully. She wants me to remember that I've been "beyond blessed" to have gotten published as much as I have and suggests I reorient my perspective. And, quite surprisingly, she suggests that I rest on my laurels—something that is not part of my nature, but that makes me pleased with what I have accomplished in the past, even though my focus is on the future.

Together we've learned that the more grateful we are for all the good in our lives, the more courageous we are when we're faced with setbacks. The glass remains half full, and we know we can fill it up when we're challenged.

Man suffers because of his craving to possess and keep forever things which are essentially impermanent . . . this frustration of the desire to possess is the immediate cause of suffering.

—*The Buddha*

10

....

Be In Touch

We are too prone to make technological instruments the scapegoats for the sins of those who wield them. The products of modern science are not in themselves good or bad, it is the way they are used that determines their value.

—*David Sarnoff*

For several years I'd lost touch with a friend who lives in Athens. Anthony used to come to New York City every few years and would call me, and we'd get together for a visit. But after Peter and I moved to Connecticut in 2007, I hadn't heard from Anthony in more than three years. A mutual friend e-mailed him and suggested he give me a call.

I was out of the cottage when Anthony called. He left his cell phone number on the answering machine. When I called him back, he yelled at me. "Sandie, for heaven's sake, I can reach anyone in the world instantaneously, but you are impossible to reach. I can't believe you don't have e-mail or at least a cell phone." After a minute, he cooled off and we had a wonderful catch-up.

I told Anthony that everyone who loves me knows how to reach me. We laughed. We go back to boarding school days and fun years in New York City when he was at Columbia University, long before cell phones and e-mail. My chosen lifestyle is too laid-back for his fast-paced personality, but we're old, good friends. And, while we couldn't see each other face-to-face, hearing each other's voices brought back a flood of good memories, and we both bragged about our adult children.

I can't even imagine how frustrating it has been for Alexandra and Brooke that I am unwilling to try some of the toys of modern life. But, with their help, my daughters and I have worked out ways for us to stay in close touch.

I still have no car. I removed the microwave oven when we renovated the cottage. We don't have a computer, and whatever model fax machine we had, I never could rely on it so I gave it away. When Brooke was pregnant, living in New York, and Peter and I were living at the Inn at Stonington, the front desk would have to try to track me down when she called because the room we were in was small, so I moved around in various spaces, often sitting out on the terrace overlooking the water in good weather. This caused my girls to waste their precious time, so I broke down, and Peter and I now have cell phones.

I really like having a cell phone because, wherever I am, my daughters can always reach me and none of us has to worry about the others unnecessarily. This is a *grace note*—a phrase I've coined to signify the instances of grace in our lives (also the name of one of my books about daily meditations that helps us to recognize this grace in our lives). I use the cell phone for one purpose only—to be in touch with Alexandra and Brooke. Period. When people inquire what my cell phone number is, I say I don't have one.

The world has embraced technology so rapidly it is hard for some people to remember using that messy black carbon paper to make a copy of a document. I can still remember paying two dollars a page to a secretary to type my first book, *Style for Living*, in the late 1960s.

When I wrote *Living a Beautiful Life*, published in the 1980s, the British company Filofax was all the rage, and I, being a lover of fine writing paper, notepads, notebooks, and stationery, became rather addicted to the wide range of paper products that fit into the six-ring personal organizer. Besides the diary and address refills, I made tabs for everything imaginable and use a variety of colors of paper; some are faintly marbleized, and some have my name printed on them. It's all great fun for me. When airlines or Amtrak or a company I'm ordering something from wants to e-mail a confirmation number, I take it over the telephone instead and put it in my Filofax. Last summer I received a Priority Mail package from Brooke with a variety of Filofax toys, including Day-Glo markers, a ruler, and a flat calculator.

Brooke knows how much I rely on this small notebook and told me I'm the only person she knows who still uses a Filofax. I'm unique!

All of us rely on different kinds of things to make our lives run smoothly. One of the great pleasures I indulge in is a birthday gift from Alexandra. She came on a plane to visit us several years ago with three young children, four suitcases, two air mattresses, and a box the size of a Xerox machine. I can't believe she made it up here in one piece from Maryland, but she did.

She explained to me why she didn't have the box shipped. "Mom, I knew you would take one look at this and be so frightened by it that you'd leave it in the box." She was right. I have a strong aversion to anything mechanical. I'm totally ignorant of how things operate. The most modern gadget I have is a fountain pen, and because it is an extension of my right arm, my pen and I get along quite well most of the time, though I've lost a lot of clothes because of ink stains.

Eventually, I got Alexandra's gift properly plugged in and up and running. It's a machine called Presto; with it, people can e-mail me, but I can't e-mail them. It's absolutely perfect. My daughters can take pictures of the grandchildren and *presto*, they come through to me as though it were a fax machine. And a grandchild can Presto me. Splendid fun, to be working away and have a ding-dong noise in the next room and hear from one of my daughters. No one can Presto me without my permission because I am in control of who knows my password. I can count the names on that list on one hand.

With the cell phone, my daughters can call me while they're waiting in a checkout line or doing a load of laundry. They both know me extremely well, and know I'm not a believer in multitasking, because it is impossible to do more than one thing at a time and be mindful; but this is the only way we can be in touch because my daughters are so busy. We do things on our own terms.

People who love their computers for work and play test my patience when they try to get me plugged in. I know my limitations, and I'm trying to be true to myself when I strictly say no to engaging in anything extra in my life that is not making me happier. I have the greatest respect for people who learn all they can from technology, but I prefer my way of living to anyone else's. We're all different. If I felt some form of technology would add to my inner peace and greatness of soul, I would be the first to embrace it. I'm keeping an open mind, but not so open my brains fall out. Efficiency and speed have their limits.

We always have things both ways. In life, we take the good and the bad. Technology doesn't engage my soul. I have human needs and sensual pleasures that are time honored, and I choose to concentrate on whatever I wish to do without someone interrupting by sending me a text message I may or may not wish to receive. I suggest a division between personal contacts and the rush of interpersonal exchanges that are under time pressure from organizations of one kind or another. There are times when we have to separate the various elements in our lives. If someone needs to reach me immediately, the telephone is the best solution.

Most people believe that advances in technology help them deal with the pressures we all have in modern life. I'm often asked what is the best way to reach me. I enjoy receiving letters. I can read them at my leisure, and am not under some false expectation to instantaneously reply. Peter and I enjoy writing letters to our children and grandchildren. We like to cut out pictures of handsome dogs from catalogs and send them to Cooper. Not everything has a deadline. Speed and efficiency are not always appropriate or graceful.

Peter was reading the book *American Lion: Andrew Jackson in the White House*, by Jon Meacham, and was interested to learn that in his retirement Jackson was restless and never slowed down. He kept up a stream of letters he called his political correspondence. Letters were his lifelines, he reported to his friends.

I acknowledge that my chosen lifestyle forces some people to write letters, get stamps, and find a mailbox. I recognize this could seem to be an imposition. While I'm sorry some friends are frustrated by my style of communication, by my saying no to a whole range of inventions and things manufactured, all the tools and gadgets available, I'm saying yes to a way of amusing and enjoying myself and finding great pleasure in the process. The prerogative of my maturity should be to be able to communicate on my own terms in the ways that seem most natural and are most appropriate for me. What fascinates me is how useful modern technology is to my life, and I am grateful that those who must use it find it quite exciting.

I love being in touch with loved ones, and everyone eventually does find me, one way or another. Aren't we fortunate? Each one of us has the freedom to choose the best possible way to live the good life and enjoy engaging with others on our own terms. Somehow, when we're kind and loving, we work things out and respect one another's different styles of communication.

Technology . . . is a queer thing. It brings you great gifts with one hand, and it stabs you in the back with the other.

—C. P. Snow

11

Never Stop Learning

It is the supreme art of the teacher to awaken joy
in creative expression and knowledge.

—Albert Einstein

Parents want the best education possible for their children. In Allan Bloom's book *The Closing of the American Mind: How Higher Education Has Failed Democracy and Impoverished the Souls of Today's Students*, published in 1987, he made a strong point about the purpose of education: "Fathers and mothers have lost the idea that the highest aspiration they might have for their children is for them to be wise—as priests, prophets or philosophers are wise. Specialized competence and success are all that they can imagine."

Parents should be proud of their children for being good, intelligent people, regardless of where they go to school. It's not where students go to learn but what they do with their education that matters. We should not simply stop educating ourselves when we get a degree.

Some children, regrettably, don't take proper advantage of their opportunities to acquire a lifelong love of learning when they are young. The most crucial thing is to impart to the young, and keep reminding ourselves of, the absolute necessity (and pleasure) of keeping one's mind open to new ideas.

I think it is important to have a sound educational base, but one doesn't necessarily have to acquire that base in a conventional way. I never went to college. But I studied hard at design school and felt the exhilaration of learning factual knowledge as well as obtaining useful skills that opened doors for me to have an exciting career as an international interior designer. That, plus the enlightening educational experience of going around the world, gave me a foundation in the pure pleasure of the learning process as well as the value of learning from travel.

In a certain sense, my lack of a college degree worked in my favor since I have always had a desire to go back and learn. For approximately half a century, I've logged in solid years of studying the remarkable lives of the greatest thinkers through the ages. My hunger and thirst for learning continues as I evolve. Whatever wisdom I have acquired along this exciting intellectual journey I owe to the brilliant minds I study. I hope I can pass on my love of learning to my family, my friends, and my readers, and trust that some of these incredibly important reflections and insights will be useful to you as you apply these lessons in your own lives. I have fallen in love with learning, and because of the stimulation I feel from various new points of view, I have grown to become more intellectually adventuresome. I continue to have fresh insights and inspiration and value this progress as my mind gains knowledge and becomes more informed.

I believe that throughout our development, in addition to a challenging academic experience, sports are a foundation to build on. The mind-body connection is what is unique to the human condition. In athletics students gain physical fitness as well as self-confidence and learn about teamwork. A healthy body best houses a healthy mind. Arts and humanities are terribly important to anyone who wants to learn how to become more cultivated. Studying the literature of ancient Greece and Rome, the classics, brings you to the source. Philosophy, the love of wisdom, concerns itself with human thought and culture. Liberal arts expose the student to refinement and appreciation of good taste and culture.

Learning and teaching are the best possible ways to spend our time. We know enough when we know and value how to learn. The learning process should be the continuous thread that gives our lives our greatest fulfillment. The time we spend studying is the essence of what we can share with others and how we can influence them in their thinking about their own lives.

If education *is* life, we should continue to study hard for the rest of our lives. The quality of learning lies within our minds. Each of us can devote ourself to the continuous rewards of evolving into a more cultured, wiser person who knows what to love and what to hate. We have to be insightful where we have the capacity to discern the true nature of reality. There is a difference between good and bad, true and false. Obviously, people have vastly different opinions and some people are stubbornly opinionated, but that doesn't mean they are correct. It's important to know what's appropriate in a situation, what is in accordance with the facts, reason, and truth. Ignorance is not an acceptable alternative. We gain profound knowledge and skill through the focused effort of studying, increasing our capacity to acquire and apply reason through the powers of our minds.

We have to become motivated to stretch our minds more vigorously, with an almost obsessive curiosity to learn, because when we are more educated, our worldview expands enormously and we experience greater pleasure in our lives. To be caught up into the world of contemplation, reasoning, and thought—that is to be educated. Throughout history human beings have evolved by thinking and expressing new ideas. We have a huge classroom—the universe. We can explore it from many different perspectives.

A lifelong love of learning begins with a love of reading. The greatest part of my educational experience is satisfied by reading books written by the brilliant minds in literature.

If parents can instill in their children a love of reading through their own example, there is a strong possibility their children will live the good life and become wiser. Alexandra and Brooke encourage their children to always bring books with them, wherever they are. When we read, we're learning, and we'll never be bored. The effort of our mental activity makes all the difference in the quality of our lives.

When Brooke and Alexandra were growing up, they observed Peter and me as avid readers. We valued reading over social life and, as a result, found great companionship as we shared long, silent evenings reading. My daughters saw, close up, how much satisfaction we gained from our reading and sharing of insights.

I admire the way Alexandra and Brooke have instilled a love of reading in their children. Tote bags full of library books come and go in their homes each week. All four grandchildren have their own libraries. Peter and I love going to bookstores with them and letting them run around selecting a bunch of books. My daughters have learned from me that having a personal library is important. You never know when just the right book is ripe to be reread.

Before Cooper turned four, at six o'clock one morning, she sat in the upstairs sitting room with me, six books in hand. "Read to me, Grand-mommy." Six books later, she scampered down to snuggle with her parents. We are a family of readers, and the joy is in the process. Without our love of reading books, our lives would be barren.

We continue to value learning because this is our ultimate source of fulfillment and pleasure, enriching every moment we live.

The aim of all education is, or should be, to teach people to educate themselves.

—Arnold Toynbee

12

....

Give Due Credit

Enthusiastic admiration is the first Principle of Knowledge.

—William Blake

Most of the good things in our lives owe something to others, and it behooves us to be consistently aware of that, even if it is not possible to thank everyone for everything. Letters, thank-you notes, timely calls, and nicely timed ceremonies are all worthwhile. Giving credit and thanks is a vital part of living well.

When I write a book, I delight in acknowledging the people who have made it possible for me to realize my dreams. In my dedications, I'm able to honor people who contribute to making my life so complete and happy. There are so many times that I'm reminded of the numerous people who have helped shape me, who have taught me, mentored me; outstanding people who set high standards of excellence for themselves and, in turn, expect a great deal from me as I strive to emulate them. There are also my good friends who make me laugh, make me think in different directions; and there are artists who show me how extraordinarily beautiful life is or can become.

There are our neighbors who go out of their way for us, acquaintances who walk their dogs and always stop to have a quick visit and a kind word. There are gardeners who have beautiful plantings in the front of their houses that we can view on our leisurely strolls through the village. I'm grateful for every detour when people tell me to go see their gardens in bloom. When we receive such abundant goodness from others, we feel an urge to praise them, to show our appreciation and recognize them in a concrete way.

I feel these inclinations not only about people who are alive and part of my daily life but also about the people from earlier generations who have died, yet who continue to guide my thinking. I dream of many of the people who have had a strong influence on me but are no longer living, and it is a comfort to me to hold them up in my mind. There is no such thing as a self-made person. We are continuously being enriched, helped, and influenced by all the stimulation around us and countless hundreds of people throughout the course of our lives.

Albert Einstein expressed in his writing deep gratitude to all the people who helped him to flourish and felt a strong obligation to give back through his work. Unless we express our thanks, how will these wonderful people know how much they contribute to our overall well-being?

If we don't like someone, for whatever reason, we can ignore him. I'm no saint, and there are some boring people and nutcases I'd just as soon not be around. But they are rare compared with the vast numbers of good people who have reached out to me in colorful, different ways, with whom I want to connect and to whom I want to express my gratitude.

My favorite way to give due credit to someone alive is to write her or him a letter. This is such an easy thing to do, and in this age of e-mail, a handwritten letter is something of a rarity and could mean more than you can possibly imagine. Someone told me recently they have my note to them on their mantel. Friends of ours have a flower business and deliver roses to us regularly. I enjoy writing a note on a floral postcard for them to pick up when the flowers are dropped off.

I've written about the power of a handwritten letter many times. In my book *Gift of a Letter*, I said a letter you send to someone you care about is a gift you give yourself. I believe this is profoundly true, because whenever you acknowledge someone in writing, you are not just recognizing his contributions to your knowledge and general pleasure but also benefiting your soul. Writing a thank-you note to someone who did something for you or who gave you a gift—the good, old-fashioned bread-and-butter letter—is good manners and is expected. But writing a kind note out of the blue will certainly surprise the recipient with joy and give you a great sense of satisfaction. The reward is well worth the effort.

Any act of kindness is always appropriate and appreciated. Whenever I receive a letter from a stranger in a faraway country, I feel the mysterious pleasure of a sense of connection. I'm fascinated when I receive a letter from a reader in Hong Kong, written to me in English, thanking me for something in one of my books that has been translated into Cantonese. These gestures have such a powerful impact because without them we never fully understand how we are influencing the lives of others.

I'm grateful that in most cases I expressed my appreciation in writing to those important people in my life who have died, or I had been in touch with them before it was too late. If one of your friends or mentors dies, it's a nice gesture to write their surviving spouse or one of their children to let them know how much you admired their loved one.

We keep these wonderful people alive by talking about them, telling their stories, recalling their passion, and recognizing all the people whose lives they've touched. One of Peter's strongest mentors was J. Edward Lumbard, a judge. Some lawyers got together and wrote a book about him after he died and have an annual dinner in his honor.

There are countless ways you can show your appreciation. It is very consoling to give credit because doing so helps the other person to understand just how deeply grateful you are. You feel an urge to recognize the generosity of spirit of the people who have helped you in large and small ways.

When you read a good book that has increased your understanding, you can recommend it to a friend. Peter practically stops people on the street to tell them to read David McCullough's superior book *The Greater Journey: Americans in Paris*. Word of mouth is effective, especially with the integrity of your recommendation. If you see a movie you enjoyed, tell a friend to go see it. I'm not usually a fan of Woody Allen, but I loved *Midnight in Paris*. I have seen it twice and tell anyone who will listen to see it if they want to have some light, fun entertainment and some good laughs. Any little connection becomes a frame of reference of a shared experience, something you now have in common.

I treasure every suggestion Alexandra and Brooke make to us. We'd owned our cottage for twenty-four years without air-conditioning. We're blessed with sea breezes and ceiling fans, and in hot spells we have additional fans on the floor and counters. When they recommended having air-conditioning in our bedroom, the nursery, and the downstairs bedroom to take the humidity out of the air when we experience extreme heat waves, it made perfect sense. It was our daughters' idea to have an outdoor shower installed in our former Zen garden so we can shower in the summer while gaping at our forest of blue hydrangea and the grandchildren can rinse off the sand from their toes after returning from the beach.

A great long-term gift to Peter and me and our family is our favorite restaurant, La Grenouille, on Fifty-second Street in New York City. I've been going there since it opened, in 1962, because my first boss, Eleanor McMillen Brown, went there with her friends and clients and often included me in the luncheon parties. Charles Masson and his mother, Madame Masson, have been so kind to us over all these years, and Peter did legal work for the restaurant. Often we've been asked, "What's your favorite restaurant in the world?" We both answer at the same time, "La Grenouille." We can go there for lunch and be in Paris without the jet lag.

Experience teaches us that there are great people in our lives who should be given credit for what they've contributed to our journeys. Call up, in your heart, all those wonderful souls who have helped you in so many ways, who have influenced you for the better. I'm sure, with some moments of deep reflection, you will come up with names of important people who will please you in your memories.

This kind of grateful recollection and reflection illuminates our paths, and our loyalty and devotion provide us with a strong sense of satisfaction and fulfillment. The more we give credit to others, the more of this goodness comes to us. It is ongoing and flows through us into others as naturally as breathing.

> *The greatest good you can do for another is not just to share your riches, but to reveal to him his own.*
>
> —*Benjamin Disraeli*

13

Keep Some Quiet Beauty
Behind Closed Doors

The reality of the building does not consist in the roof and walls,
but in the space within to be lived in.

—*Lao Tzu*

When I raised Alexandra and Brooke, anything attractive that I owned I
had on display. Because I was an interior designer, our home doubled as a
decorator's show house. But with toddlers, I constantly had to say,
"Pretty, don't touch." I wanted them to admire the beauty but not destroy
it. Now I want our grandchildren to have full run of our cottage and have
surfaces they can put to continuous good use. I wanted to make the cottage atmosphere feel young and inviting for our family and stimulating
for us.

Just as with a secret garden, I've come to discover it is extremely satisfying and important for us to have personal spaces and treasures that are
meant for our private delight. Not everything in a well-lived life is meant

to be shared, nor is it appropriate to have all the objects we own on permanent display. The opening and closing of doors as a way of living has become an exhilarating transformation for me at this stage in our lives.

The lovely paradox about the beauty behind closed doors is the inexplicable delight when we open a cabinet door and see with fresh eyes the pretty objects we love. Nothing looks tired. Even though closing off beauty sounds counterintuitive, and certainly conflicts with friends' expectations, everyone who knows me understands I love pretty things. By putting our rooms on a diet, by creating a feeling of expansiveness, we let our rooms feel fresh and young, and, as a result, so do we. The notion that things can and should be hidden (though not always, of course) works well for us and provides enormous freedom and flexibility.

In order to renovate and paint the cottage, we had to empty it. The sheer unadorned beauty of the spaces made us acutely aware of how important it is for us to keep the rooms clean, spare, uncluttered, and pure. This is such a reversal from the way we lived before the renovation that there are moments when I can't believe I'm the same person I was then. In reality I'm not. With clean windows, we feel a deeper connection with our garden, the harbor, and nature, and we have achieved something even greater—we now feel a deep sense of inner peace.

Most people who love to read feel most comfortable in spaces crowded with books. I don't. I remember waking up one morning in our New York City apartment bedroom and feeling that the wall of books was threatening. I'd read some but not all of them, and we had a library down the hall. I removed the bookcases in the bedroom and created a charming sitting area with a large painting of sky and water that brought me great pleasure and a sense of calm.

All of us learn about our emotional comfort over time. We've all had tingles; particular moments when we're aware that our place is just right for us and the light, the mood, the colors in our spaces bring us absolute delight.

Several things led me to my fresh vision. After our friend and favorite artist Roger Mühl suddenly died several years ago, I wanted our cottage to be spare in order to not distract the eye from his colorful, life-enhancing paintings. Peter's second knee operation led us to having fewer possessions around that could be tripped over. And now that I'm no longer an interior designer, I have a different point of view about our home.

There are private joys involved in collecting things you love over the years. And if you're fortunate enough to travel about and bring back things you are fond of, your surroundings become your autobiography. Over the years, however, especially if you live to old age, your house can become cluttered and can feel old.

After our cottage renovation, I needed pure space to relax my mind. I craved emptiness. I wanted to feel serene. When I first went to Japan, I was a teenager and was studying interior design. I discovered that the Japanese have a philosophy of leaving certain shelves empty in order to have space to breathe. I didn't put anything back on the freshly painted shelves in the two living rooms, in the study, or in the back hall. The back of each shelf had been painted a glorious shade of blue that echoes the blue sky of a perfect sunny day in Stonington, with the freshest sea air.

Later, I had a change of heart from wanting empty shelves to wanting to make room for some beautiful objects. So to maintain the atmosphere of peaceful calm, I decided to have all the open shelves in the downstairs of the cottage concealed by cabinet doors. We can arrange our beautiful objects on the shelves without cluttering our spaces.

As soon as Mike, our favorite carpenter, installed our cabinet doors, I knew I was onto something important. All ages can share the rooms together and feel the comfort of having spaces to engage in their own activities. Our cottage is young, light, bright, and ready for anything. When Cooper comes she immediately opens some lower cabinet doors in the living room and sets up her toys to play. Things come out and go back onto the shelves effortlessly. There is quiet beauty behind closed doors because they have expanded our visual spaces, brought organization to our everyday life, and protected everything from dust, making my lungs extremely happy. And, as the spirit moves me, I can easily bring out any of our pretty objects and place them around. Our rooms feel crisp and modern, and because they are clean and lean, they're able to adapt instantly to any situation. I enjoy the sense of privacy as well as the mystery of not exposing everything all at once.

Even the buttery off the kitchen is beautiful, with our favorite small paintings and glass vases and pitchers for arranging flowers. I'm constantly rearranging things that delight us, and when we choose to, we open the door and cabinets to feast our eyes.

There aren't any stuffy, stiff, or staid displays around. All our books are upstairs in my writing room, in Peter's library–writing room, and on our fun third floor, off-limits to everyone except us and our grandchildren.

As Brooke likes to say, fun is free. Now, the whole cottage is ready for fun. As it turns out, the third floor is all four grandchildren's favorite space. There are so many reasons why this is true. After all, it is an attic and is totally private and relaxed.

In the back, there is an art room with an art table and individual desks. Art and craft supplies are stored in a chartreuse filing cabinet with labeled drawers. Each child has her or his own drawer to store personal projects. The walls are silver insulation board, and we tape up the kids' artwork, framing it with silver tape. We had the chimney walled over in order to put up a huge mirror for ballet practice and Irish dance. Large plastic shelves house books, framed photographs, and boxes full of fun things to play with.

Peter and I go to "three" every afternoon to be utterly private; it is another place to study, to write and muse, looking over memorabilia, our archives, paintings, and treasured objects.

We're free to open what's closed and close what's open. There's beauty in this concept, I assure you.

Every wall is a door.

—*Ralph Waldo Emerson*

14

....

Guard What You Say

I am very little inclined on any occasion to say anything
unless I hope to produce some good by it.

—*Abraham Lincoln*

Sometimes the less you say, the kinder and wiser you are. Free advice may cost you a strain in a relationship, and we usually don't have enough concrete knowledge to give a well-informed opinion about a situation without studying the facts. Rarely do my daughters ask for my advice, although they sometimes use me as a sounding board. The more I listen, the less I have to say.

All of us have said things we regret, but we should seriously try not to, because we don't want to hurt someone else's feelings. And few of us appreciate getting caught up in trivial conversations. Sometimes, people pour their guts out, telling you much more than you want to know about their intimate family dynamics or the abrupt reversal of their financial situations. We don't want to be insensitive, but this kind of sharing is definitely inappropriate. The secret of not being a bore, I believe, is not to tell everything.

Even when you're saying something nice and complimenting someone, it can be misunderstood, especially in family situations. Fifty years ago I told my brother-in-law that he was the best thing that ever happened to my sister. I've been punished for this remark ever since. You may not be gossiping but caring, but you can end up saying something you wouldn't want repeated to the person you are talking about because it would hurt their feelings.

Be mindful of what you tell others about yourself, your life, your friends, or your enemies. A well-known judge and Peter's mentor John Marshall Harlan coached young lawyers this way: "I want to tell you right away about how to behave. When you say something you think, it's the same thing as you carrying the message to the front page of the *New York Times*." Good, sound advice. Don't say anything that you truly do not wish repeated. People take your words out of context. In this age of information, discretion is essential. A friend of mine gave her best friend an expensive necklace for Christmas. The best friend returned it for a store credit rather than let it sit in a drawer. But the saleswoman told the buyer it had been returned, causing the friendship to end and the employee to lose her job.

Silence *is* sometimes golden. Best to think, and talk only to yourself about so many aspects of your life. Guard what you say in order to prevent indiscretion. What happens when we hear about a problem? We automatically give advice, hoping to offer some perspective in order that a solution can be found. But often, we end up putting our feet in our mouths because our advice falls on deaf ears and might even be misunderstood. And, once said, our words could be repeated to others. When someone complains to me about something, I have the bad habit of telling the story of a worse problem, turning the conversation into a downward spiral. Silence can be golden.

A good rule of thumb is not to listen to secrets or tell them. Everyone has to work out their own problems the best they can. It's inappropriate to talk about things of an intimate nature with people who are not involved in the issue. No one should know details about another person's relationships. And a half-truth is just that, a half-truth. It is disloyal to the trust and confidence and love bond to tell others secrets that should be kept private. Assume most people can't keep a secret and you'll be better off. Exercise restraint and be careful whom you trust. Confidential matters should be kept hidden from others. Remember how rumors start. Someone blabs to someone else about someone else.

As a mother and stepmother, I'd prefer not to be in the middle of a situation where I am expected to choose sides. Parents shouldn't be put in a position that will in any way jeopardize their meaningful relationship with their children, no matter what age. A maxim that everyone knows but few people pay attention to is, "We seldom regret talking too little, but very often regret talking too much." You will never say something inappropriate when you bite your lip and remain silent.

Situations are dynamic, ever changing. What you say one day will be quite different in the future, and when you give too much information in the heat of passion, or out of anguish or frustration, the person you confide in will be worrying about you long after your circumstances have improved, along with your mood.

Of course, friends sometimes need us to act as sounding boards, but when we deeply love someone and learn that someone else is hurting her, we become fiercely protective and, without knowing both sides of the story, we tend to judge the other person wrongly. We shouldn't be put in a position where we become so frustrated that we say bad things about anyone. Quite frankly, no one wants to hear about someone's deep, dark secrets unless they can do something useful to help when they receive the information. If someone comes to you genuinely seeking your advice, trusting in your judgment, that is a different story.

Whatever the situation, think long and hard about giving advice. Almost never do so unless you are asked. Peter has a lawyer friend who feels compelled to tell you exactly what's on his mind. Once he told me that I spend too much time with Peter. Another time, at a black-tie dinner, he told me I shouldn't wear pantsuits. Free advice is usually cheap. It is better not to express your feelings unless asked, although everyone is entitled to their own thoughts. Even thoughtful people who have a great deal to say are most often wise not to give unsolicited advice.

When you *are* asked to give advice, make sure that you know what is expected. Often people simply want to be reassured about the wisdom of their own decisions. But there are times when the asker really needs the best advice that you can give. Know the difference. And there are other times when someone simply needs to vent frustration about a boss or spouse or child. They need your ear, not your advice.

When a friend tells me something seriously sad about her life, my typical reaction is to hug her and let her talk to me. Often I don't have anything to say other than "I'm sorry" or "I love you." But even then, I don't want my friend to feel sorry for herself. I want to cheer her up, give her hope and strength. After sad information has been shared, it is often wisest not to bring it up again. The mutual knowledge and understanding is there. In deeply serious times, we may have nothing appropriate to say. There are times when we are in pain and we are called upon to be courageous. The loving support of family and friends helps us to make the best of whatever circumstances we have to face.

I say this with a great deal of thought because when someone is weighted down by the pain of her situation, and feels it is important for you to know what she is struggling with, silence is usually the best response. Loved ones know you love them, and when someone is deeply hurting, you want to reach out to her in loving, life-enhancing ways.

Awful, awful things happen to good, decent people, and they need all the brave bones in their beings to overcome their suffering. Kindness, compassion, tenderness, and the grace of your companionship will encourage their bravery and commitment to overcome whatever the situation may be. Being fully present and nonjudgmental in delicate circumstances is wise. Sometimes I become choked up and simply tell people, "I have nothing to say."

Another important aspect of remaining quiet is that people aren't always ready to hear the truth. We all engage in denial to varying degrees, depending on our temperaments. But adults have to make the necessary tough choices and live with the consequences. No one can make these decisions for someone else. However, when someone genuinely is seeking your advice, you can suggest options; ask the right questions that will help the person come to the proper decision on his own.

The University of Ottawa offers a useful tool, a "decision guide" that includes detailed questions to help people weigh the pros and cons of any type of decision. If someone calls on you to give serious advice, have the person asking for your help do her research. Have her write down the possible or probable answers to her questions. Ideally, with your support and encouragement, the one asking for your advice will be able to come to the right conclusion.

There are certain realities people are just not ready to face. I admit I don't always see the worst-case scenario, but all of us will be better able to face our most difficult choices with the help and clarity of someone whose wise judgment informs us.

Some things are just not our business, even if they are our concern. An accountant told me a horror story of a corrupt, dishonest client, and because he never asked me for my advice, I remained silent. But I am concerned that by keeping the client on, he is doing something for money that is against his better judgment.

We can only hear what we can understand, and understanding requires acceptance. When my best friend suddenly became very ill, she couldn't accept or understand the specific details of her illness. She was told she got sick from the fertilizer in her garden. This could be true. Who knows? It certainly is possible these toxic chemicals were the cause of her illness. However, it wasn't until Tess was transferred from a general hospital to a cancer hospital that she knew, for sure, she had cancer.

When someone asks me, "Do you want me to tell you what I think?" the answer is, "It depends." Often I choose not to hear someone's opinion if I don't feel they are going to be tactful. Tact is extremely important in our interactions with others. When we are acutely sensitive to what is proper and appropriate in our relationships, we will be able to speak and act without offending. We should strive to never hurt anyone. Aim to be considerate as well as discreet. If someone asks me something inappropriate, my answer is, "I'll never tell." Living well requires diplomacy, a certain skill and adroitness in managing awkward situations. We are not born with social intelligence; we learn it through our interactions with others, starting in early childhood.

There are wonderful people who have the grace and savoir faire, the knack and tact, to say the right thing. I was told growing up, If you can't say something nice, don't say anything at all. What right does a person have to hurt someone else's feelings? We have a friend who enjoyed hanging out in a local restaurant until a regular customer there said something to her that deeply hurt her feelings. As a consequence, she won't go there anymore. She doesn't go into any details, she simply says, "Whatever," with a shrug. The person that said something indiscreet doesn't even know the harm he caused our sensitive friend.

We should continue to be careful about what we say because it can, and often will, be used against us. Unfortunately, too many times we're not really at liberty to say what we think and feel. Think of the careers that have been ruined by people talking too much. When Peter is asked something he doesn't want to talk about, he jokes, "When I told you hello, I told you all I know."

Peter and I share a private code: When either one of us is tempted to say something disparaging or disrespectful, we use our code to not open our mouth. The old saying—if you can't say something nice, don't say anything at all—really does help us not to belittle others. Think whatever you like, but don't say something insensitive that will hurt another's feelings.

When asked for advice, be extremely thoughtful about what you say. Don't say too much. Most often, I've come to understand from experience, the less said *is* the better.

Those who know do not talk and talkers do not know.

—*Lao Tzu*

15

....

Choose to Remain an Optimist

The basic belief that leads to optimism, remember,
is that setbacks or failures are due to circumstances that we can do
something about to change them for the better.

—*Daniel Goleman*

Dare to be an optimist.

It is better by far to take an optimistic view than a pessimistic one: a valuable lesson that life and my daughters have taught me.

No matter what has happened to me that was tragic or that caused me to become sad or discouraged, I've always bounced back relatively quickly. It is well-known that optimism creates more good than pessimism. We all need the encouragement hope brings us. Peter believes that "hope alone can sustain us, especially when optimism is on our side." All achievements involve expectations that we wish to be fulfilled. We look forward with confidence and expect that things will work out according to our plans and, if not, that we will find a way to move forward until we see favorable results.

All of humanity will still have children and expect pleasure and some deep gratification and love from them. We hope they will be successful and live good lives. And while our children's world is greatly different from ours, largely because of the advances in technology, human beings have always had an extraordinary capacity to adapt to change, continuously seeking prosperity and progress and pleasure over pain. We all need food, desire sex, and care for our children, but there is a world of difference between the way we and our children think and do everything in all the varied facets of our lives.

Optimism increases our strength and focus, allowing us to become more effective and to triumph. Without the sense that we will be able to win out over whatever odds we face, we'd give up. Hope is a shining star in a dark night, cheering us up when we face setbacks, when the wind is no longer at our backs. But we must sail on and be hopeful, because optimism produces the power to bring us safely to shore.

The mother of friends of ours was diagnosed with breast cancer. The first thing she said was "Let's get on with this because I'm playing in a tennis tournament in a month." My immediate thought when I heard she was going in for an operation was sadness that she had to suffer. Surrounded by her loving family and friends, she lived life to the hilt, did what she had to do, and moved on. The morning after her procedure, she was doing her usual power walk with one of her daughters. Bobette is an inspiration to us all. Off to Texas she went to win the Senior Olympics tennis tournament.

A local musician, Charles Holland, is loved by our community. He plays and sings in a jazz band at a local seaside restaurant Sunday afternoons, as well as at weddings and charity events. He played in Brooke's wedding, to the delight of all the generations. A few years ago the town threw a surprise party to celebrate Charles's eighty-fifth birthday. He seemed really touched by the turnout of over two hundred.

The following year he began to slow down; he lost his spunk and didn't feel well. There were several brief trips to the hospital, some extended hospital stays, and three operations (or "procedures," as he would say with a wink). He spent months in a rehabilitation facility. The rumor was that he'd checked out, his time was up, he was ready to die. Peter and I feared we'd never see him again.

Wrong. On his eighty-sixth birthday, Charles showed up at a favorite restaurant with one of his brothers, looking ten years younger, trim, and healthy. He's back cracking jokes, telling stories about being a bomber in World War II in Europe, discussing the books he's reading, and singing and playing, fully engaged in life. The great lesson I learned from his remarkable reversal of health is to never give up on anyone. The human spirit, our life force, is strong.

We have the will to believe we can improve our condition. The surprising effectiveness of placebos may be proof of the indomitable, unalterable optimism in our hearts and souls. The profound value of daring to be an optimist is that human intelligence systematically prefers the positive good over the negative bad. We all wish for happy endings, but if a happy ending isn't realistic, we should at least insist on the journey being uplifting and exhilarating, and insist on the best possible quality of life for ourselves. Optimism has the power of healing us even if it can't always cure us. The cells in our bodies immediately respond to the thoughts in our minds. There is no disconnect.

Humor helps get our spirits headed in the right direction. There are times to be deadly serious and realistic, but there are other times to joke around and have some lighthearted fun with friends no matter how dire a situation appears to be. We're in charge of setting the tone of our lives. If our basic background attitude is optimistic, we will live in the sunlight and not the shadow. There will never be a situation we can't improve as long as we live. This understanding should inspire and encourage our higher power of strength and resourcefulness. We need never lose our perspective or our love of life.

We're continuously gaining when we adopt the optimistic strength to live as fully as possible given our circumstances. Look all around at signs of people's faith in the ability to embrace whatever we choose to accomplish. Look at a cathedral and remember that it began with a pile of rocks and a spirit of optimism. It is a grace note. Think of the great achievements that can come from group optimism while never underestimating the vision of each individual with positive spirit.

When our spirit-energy is optimistic, it provides the stimulus for improving the world together, one step at a time, good deed by good deed. In times of great challenge, everyone must have a noble character. For the world order to improve, we must believe we have the capacity and drive to make a difference. Hope, optimism, and love are necessary in every condition. I choose to remain an optimist. Both of my daughters enthusiastically embrace the opportunity to make a difference, and thoughtfully live with this commitment.

When you do the work necessary to clean your conscience, then the joy of living returns and the physiology of optimism restores you.

—Bernie Siegel

16

....

Know What to Look for in a Husband and What to Work Toward in a Marriage

If only we could all accept that there is no difference between us where human values are concerned. Whatever sex.

—*Liv Ullmann*

Daughters as well as mothers have husbands. We're all in this together. While everyone is different, there are certain common characteristics of good marriages. What should a woman look for in a husband? What should she expect?

At a book event recently, I asked the audience if they had any ideas for subjects they wanted me to cover in my new book. One woman suggested I write a whole book about marriage. I was delighted to hear this suggestion, and it led to a lively discussion. Most of the people in the room were women, and some of them suggested I use Peter as an example to help instruct husbands.

It was flattering, and the idea stayed in my mind. I realized that Peter is as good a human being as can be and as fine a husband as anyone could dream of sharing their life with. He calls me "angel" in public. We still hold hands. He is quick to compliment me on the way I look, as well as about the way I conduct my life.

For years women have told us they're looking for someone just like Peter. Male friends tell us they are better husbands after spending time with Peter. Peter spends his life trying to please me. I find this man I love so much to be dependably easygoing and fun to be with. Peter was my inspiration to write *Happiness for Two: 75 Secrets for Finding More Joy Together.* In his ninetieth year, at the suggestion of David Brooks, Peter wrote an op-ed piece in the *New York Times* called "The Life Report." He wrote, "From the beginning, I was a happy man, and enjoyed *every* day. As I look back now, I feel that I have been given the most enjoyable times possible for any human life, although some of it wasn't exactly easy."

Peter has always wanted me to fulfill myself and live up to my potential. He continuously encourages me, and shows his deep affection and pride when I work hard and achieve results.

On the back cover of *Happiness for Two* are my words: "Happiness for two requires two sensitive, loving souls who understand their own potential for wholeness individually. The more we love our own life, the more we inspire and strengthen our partner's journey. When we love with this loving kindness, patience, and wisdom, we will find great happiness." I am married to an accomplished, fulfilled, happy man. Peter exudes happiness and everyone who comes in contact with him feels his loving, gentle spirit.

It happens that Peter is rarely cranky. His disposition is the result of a combination of good qualities I greatly admire—he is disciplined, strong, sensitive, and affectionate, and, at the same time, understanding and accepting. I think about this a lot because when a husband is moody, the entire atmosphere becomes toxic. Obviously, the same holds true for a wife or child or friend being in a bad mood; as we all know, this creates tension, and a negative disposition becomes contagious. No matter what happens at the workplace, husbands should try to come home with grateful hearts. The paradox is that no one can make another person happy, but unhappy people can affect the inner peace and serenity of those they are closest to. Because Peter and I now spend most of our time together, I am especially appreciative of his admirable strength of character and temperament. He is basically cheerful.

Good husbands have to have great character. When you are considering marrying someone, ask yourself, Who is this person, really? How strong are his inner resources? Is he emotionally healthy? Is he gentle and kind? Is he thoughtful and understanding? What a husband wishes for in his life should be the same as what his wife wants in hers. The only difference between a man and a woman, fundamentally, is the way each one contributes to the next generation. We share the same basic needs and should have similar values. The finer someone's character, the better the quality of his or her relationships. Only good people enjoy the good life.

Some people believe men and women are entirely different, but I disagree. Society has programmed us differently, but we are especially alike in our feelings, our passions, and our desires to love and be loved. In my daughters' generation I see a healthy shift toward women being more revered in our male-dominated culture. We will all live in greater harmony when we are not divided into a patriarchal or a matriarchal society. Obviously, husbands should honor and obey their wives with the same reverence, tenderness, and respect as wives revere their husbands. When two people equally look up to each other, expect a successful relationship. There should be no hierarchy in authority or status. We should seek a balance in which each person is appreciated for his or her individual contributions.

The honesty and sharing of responsibilities in modern marriages is extremely refreshing, and it encourages wives who want to make something of their own lives. In past generations, wives had to play roles that were assumed and not necessarily chosen. Why was it that women were expected to manage the finances, decorate and maintain the house, cook, take care of the children, be responsible for everyone's social life, and plan the vacations? It's far better when these tasks are shared with a sense of mutual respect, pleasure, and companionship.

Husbands often have to be reminded that women want the same freedom to choose how to live satisfying lives that men have, and there should not be any gender assumptions. Rather than asking "What's for dinner?" a husband could say, "What do you think we should do about dinner tonight?" A good husband will never take advantage of his spouse's good nature. A wife might love to cook, but not every night on command.

Husbands who take turns helping with the laundry, dishwashing, cooking, cleaning, and child care are valuing their wives' time. When a husband offers to help and is willing to be pressed into service, this is a great comfort to his wife, who may be short of time. A hug or a kiss and a genuinely generous offer to be useful—"What can I do for you right now?"—are great stress reducers and true signs of affection. When Peter spontaneously rubs my shoulders, I say, "More." And out of compassion he spends a few more moments to help me relax. Sometimes when I feel pressured, he'll remind me to take my time and not rush. Often his patience has the power to soothe my nerves.

Husbands need to know how to communicate well about everything involving their wives and families. They should never, ever agree to go anywhere their wives or children are expected to attend without first discussing it with their wives. Nothing is worse than for a wife to learn about some command performance at a family reunion or office party without having been able to talk about the decision to attend together. Avoid unnecessary misunderstandings by having regular, honest communications about your mutual lives.

Husbands should always ask. I repeat, don't assume a darn thing. It is entirely unfair to assume another person's availability. Don't invite someone to your house without checking with your wife. She could have a mud pack on her face. Home should be private, and guests should come only by the invitation of both partners in the marriage. If Peter doesn't want to do something, unless it is urgently important to me, we don't do it. I respect his limitations. When there are sensitive issues to decide, sit down and talk things over so you both can have a give-and-take in the discussion, face-to-face. Don't send an e-mail. Allow enough uninterrupted time to come to a resolution.

Sometimes husbands forget they are no longer bachelors. Husbands shouldn't make any firm business plans without first discussing them with their wives. If you do plan a business trip, check with your wife immediately to be sure the timing is appropriate for the family. When there is mutual love and respect, this continuous exchange of thoughts and plans avoids unnecessary tension. Even if a husband wants to do something with a friend without inviting his wife to participate, the spouses should work things out together, providing mutual support. The timing of his plans could be crucial to her appointments, commitments, and deadlines.

Before being married, we're free to come and go as we wish, doing things spontaneously, playing things by ear. However, when two people are involved, life operates on a schedule, and once you have children, planning ahead is crucial. Doing things on the spur of the moment causes great stress, takes more time and effort, and is invariably more expensive. Last-minute thoughts might be romantic, but you still have to make arrangements for a babysitter, a dog sitter, or travel plans. If you book a reservation earlier, you can save serious money. To never know what her husband is doing makes it difficult for a wife to plan ahead. And thinking in advance adds to your pleasure by allowing you to anticipate an enjoyable event.

A husband should be more of a sensualist when you are together. It is insulting to a woman for her husband to bring his technology to the table or, worse, to the bedroom. Peter and I were in a restaurant where, at every table in sight, people were playing with their gadgets. Men *and* women. I find this rude. Turn it all off and have the grace and discipline to make certain moments sacrosanct, where nothing is more important than the two of you being on a date. Have someone from the office cover for you. You can't be on call for others twenty-four hours a day and also be a caring, sensitive, loving husband. Your wife wants you to be responsive to her feelings, and she needs you to pay attention to her, with eye contact, when you are alone together. Time is precious, and when you listen well and ask thoughtful, intimate questions, the quality of your experiences alone together will be greatly magnified and more constructive.

There is no feeling sadder than the loneliness a wife can feel if her husband is in denial about problems in their relationship. A woman doesn't want to talk things out with a good friend; she wants to have a heart-to-heart with her husband because he is meant to be her best friend. The way for a husband to be his wife's best friend is to put her well-being before his, and that is what she should do for her husband as well. Just as a wife wants her husband to fulfill himself, this should be a husband's primary concern for the woman he married.

I can assure every husband that unless he is completely supportive of his wife's creative, evolving journey, she will act out in unusual, awkward ways as an escape from the pain of not being free to develop and use her God-given talents and passionately pursue her interests.

I have some male friends who think I can, at times, be too hard on men. I've even been accused of "male-bashing." While I love being a woman, I can't imagine how impoverished I'd be without my love of men. The advice I have for husbands is sound, solid, and serious. They can't keep a good woman down. Husbands won't learn these lessons at Harvard Business School, and they can't use their own fathers or grandfathers or uncles as role models because times have changed and the way those earlier generations behaved was not the example modern husbands need. Peter's father was not allowed in the kitchen, and Peter has made it clear to me he has no interest in cooking. His generation got away with this behavior. But younger husbands must share in the domestic responsibilities or they will suffer.

Basically, a husband will be right to assume that what he wants is what his wife wants. The glue that keeps a marriage together is mutual respect and devotion.

Husbands, ask yourselves: What do I most want for my wife? Love and happiness, also courage and clarity, inner peace, joy, vibrant health, intimacy, harmonious relationships, faith, hope, and passion. You want her to express herself and feel the pleasure of loving her work. You want her to feel your love and caring support.

Husbands can answer this question in their own words. I asked Peter what he wants *for* me, and this was his response:

- *Love*
- *Happiness*
- *Health*
- *Creativity*
- *Passion*
- *Mental stimulation*
- *Time with my children and grandchildren*
- *Being up-to-date with world affairs*
- *Looking and feeling attractive*
- *Financial security*
- *A beautiful environment*
- *Freedom to develop my potential*
- *Fresh flowers*

What interests me is that love is always the first word that comes to mind when Peter and I think of each other and what we most value in our lives.

This exercise took less than ten minutes, and Peter said it was fun. He added a few minutes later, looking up from the book he was reading, "Darling, I want you to have a bright and happy future." He was on a roll, so I went to his desk, sat opposite him, and asked, "What do you, as my husband, want *from* me?"

Peter's response:

- *Love*
- *Trust*
- *Faithfulness*
- *Forgiveness*
- *Understanding*
- *Integrity*
- *Caring*
- *Generosity*
- *Character*

- *Kindness*
- *Cheerfulness*
- *Affection*
- *Appreciation*
- *Companionship*
- *Intimacy*
- *Friendship*
- *Sense of humor*
- *Patience*

These words are listed as Peter spoke in stream of consciousness. By asking yourself what you wish *for* your spouse, and then what you want *from* your husband or wife, you will see with clarity how crucially important it is to your union to not be a hypocrite in your thoughts, words, and deeds, expecting what you are unwilling to give. Confucius believed that "the way of a superior man is three-fold: Virtuous, he is free from anxieties; wise, he is free from perplexities; bold, and he is free from fear."

I believe this is what we all want in a husband and what I want from my husband—for him to be virtuous, wise, and bold, a mirror of what I want for myself. This is an honorable goal and what we should work toward in an ideal marriage. A good marriage is a process of learning to love truth, to love yourself, to love your partner as your other half, and to value the dignity of each soul as sacred as you evolve together into the fullness of your powers.

There are thousands of little ways we show our love and respect for the most important people in our lives, our husbands or our wives. My wish list is long, and admittedly my standards are high, but happiness is an elusive achievement and is hard earned, especially when intimacy and confidences are shared over a long marriage. Once husbands get into the swing of doing the right thing, at the right time, for the right reason, the cultivation of their character will shine through their behavior and they will be a big part of creating healthy, harmonious, and happy marriages. Time helps teach us the lessons that are most useful to know.

The wisdom we want our husbands to acquire is the same we wives want. While we will express our love and consideration differently, by wanting our spouse to flourish, to evolve and become self-actualized, we have to want the same thing for ourselves. The same goes, without saying, for our children. We teach through example. I have tried to show Alexandra and Brooke how necessary it is for women to fulfill themselves and have their own identities and meaningful work. My daughters thoroughly understand this important advice. A genuinely happy marriage is the best possible role model for friends and family; without a positive example of a happy marriage, children are at a disadvantage, no matter what other positive influences there are in their lives. Because Peter is naturally so supportive of me in all my interests and activities, my daughters have seen up close how such caring brings contentment, a sense of purpose, and great satisfaction.

If you want your husband to watch less television, don't watch it yourself. If you like watching the nightly news together, enjoy the companionship and then turn the television off before dinner. If you want to encourage your spouse to read more books by highly intelligent, serious writers, read more good authors yourself, sharing your books and insights. If you want your husband to be more meticulous in his grooming and his appearance, let him model your style and behavior. If you want your husband to be neat, keep a well-ordered house. If you want your husband to have better lifestyle habits, improve your own and encourage any baby steps in a healthier direction. Live by the Golden Rule.

Keep in mind that everything is reciprocal. There must be a continuous, mutual, and cooperative exchange of favors. A successful marriage requires give and take, sharing in the responsibilities and in the joy of commitment, devotion, and companionship as confidants. You will share secrets and all kinds of private matters that, out of loyalty, you would never disclose to anyone else. The noble character trait of discretion brings harmony to an intimate relationship.

Lord knows, we all have faults, but a long time ago, Horace (best known for having taught us to seize the day, *carpe diem*) understood that the "man is best who has fewest." None of us are perfect, but for the most part, we care and we try. And, for a number of reasons, even when we try our best, some things just happen, and they require us to take a deep breath, stay calm, and face the situation head-on. Remember to keep these awkward moments to yourself. Certain things are private. When we are in an intimate, loving marriage, we need to be understanding of our own shortcomings as well as the faults of our spouses.

One of the nicest things about Peter's nature is his generosity of spirit in showing appreciation for all the good he feels I do, and for the joy and pleasure he feels. The more he expresses his appreciation, the more motivated I am to go out of my way to create a loving atmosphere for our daily lives under all circumstances. Feeling appreciated is a great motivator and keeps me from becoming discouraged when there is a rough patch to face.

My advice to wives: Never let your husband outgrow you intellectually or emotionally. Both partners need to be equally intellectually stimulating in order to continue to be compatible. Never sell yourself short. Always have your own voice to create your story. Have interests and talents that will sustain you throughout your life. Jacqueline Kennedy embarked on a career as a book editor at Doubleday, after her second husband, Aristotle Onassis, the Greek shipping magnate, died. She told a friend she had come to realize she could not expect to live primarily through a husband. We cannot live through each other. We are meant to both live, *with* each other, being neither onlookers nor bystanders. It takes two to tango.

I feel Peter and I were meant to be together as lifelong partners. Both Alexandra and Brooke have been under Peter's loving influence as their adoring stepfather for most of their lives, and I'm certain they have learned wise lessons from him that they can apply to their own marriages. We all share a love of celebrations, creating as many wonderful memorable experiences as possible. My daughters definitely follow my advice to remember that life is short, and none of us take anything for granted.

Peter's and my example of having fun together is something both my daughters embrace, and they approach their marriages with this attitude of pleasure in the process of living and loving together.

> *Love does not consist in gazing at each other but in*
> *looking outward together in the same direction.*
>
> —Antoine de Saint-Exupéry

17

Give Back

The law of living is giving
The nature of nature is giving
The clouds are giving rain
Trees are giving fruit
Earth is giving grain
Sun is giving warmth
Moon and stars are giving light
With gifts of nature's giving, we are living
to complete the cycle of living and giving
Let us give from our mind, hands and heart
to the world

—Chitrabhanu

The world owes us nothing. We owe our life to the world, and must give back for the gift of being alive. Recently I was having a deeply reflective discussion with a friend a few weeks after the sudden death of his wife.

The conversation drifted into the topic "What is the meaning of life?" Irvin laughed and said, "Enjoy life to the hilt and be good." Be good, do good, and you will be happy.

Throughout life we can continuously find ways to serve that will make the sayings we were raised with ring true: "It is better to give than to receive" and "When much has been given, much is expected." The greatest lesson to learn is how to be good. We are good by doing good, by serving others. We receive by giving of ourselves from our hearts to others. Showing our thanks and appreciation is a gift we give ourselves. There are hundreds of small day-to-day things we can do to show our gratitude. Something as simple as a smile and a sincere compliment can mean so much to someone who might not feel well or who is in emotional pain. When you get a restaurant check, you can write a short note of thanks to the waiter if you enjoyed the meal and service. This, along with a generous tip, is a grace note that will be appreciated. Giving is an attitude and a process that is the key to happiness.

Brooke reads Beliefnet newsletters—Daily Buddhist Wisdom—and when there's something she really loves, she sends it along to me. Here's an example:

Don't be afraid of doing good.
It's another name for happiness,
for all that is dear and delightful—this phrase "doing good."
Whoever would live well, Long lasting, bringing bliss—Let him be generous,
be calm,
And cultivate the doing of good. By practicing these three,

These three bliss-bringing things, The wise one lives without regret.
His world infused with happiness.

—Itivuttaka Sutta

Overall, American individuals are exceedingly generous and raise enormous amounts of money for worthy causes. Not only do they give money but they volunteer, performing service of their own free will. What sort of giving do you like to do? What do your friends do? Volunteerism is what makes communities thrive, especially in economic hard times. Our local firemen are volunteers, and so are many of the ambulance drivers. What are some of your favorite ways to volunteer? A friend of mine drives a woman in a wheelchair to her doctors' appointments. Another friend visits a bedridden elderly woman and reads to her.

One of the most endearing things Peter did recently was to raise more than $17,000 for our local library's Children's Room, which was flooded in a bad storm in 2010 and had all its books ruined. The following July Fourth weekend, when all four grandchildren were here, under Brooke and Alexandra's supervision, they set up a lemonade stand and baked cupcakes. It was Cooper's idea, because she was at her grandfather Peter Rabbit's eight-hour book signing two summers before, and she wanted to give the library more money. (Our grandchildren's nickname for Peter is Peter Rabbit—the naughty bunny!) Cooper goes to various programs in the Children's Room and loves meeting new friends there.

Anna, Lily, Nicholas, and Cooper vigorously announced to the passing crowds and cars, "Ice-cold lemonade and homemade cupcakes—twenty-five cents." Nicholas shouted into a makeshift megaphone, "All money goes to the Stonington Free Library for the Children's Room." Alexandra wanted to know how I felt about noise control, and I assured her our neighbors would be delighted to come over and make a contribution so that the children would see the success of their efforts.

By pure chance, the sailing school classes at the yacht club down the block got out just then and everyone was hungry and thirsty. Often when the children were making change, people would say, "Keep it. And keep up your good work."

I saw a friend give five dollars, and another friend driving by said she'd never seen Peter and me smile so broadly. This scene is one of the sweetest moments I will cherish in my memory.

The stand was such a success that the children wanted to do it again the next day. They were having so much fun. These four entrepreneurs, ages two and a half, seven, nine, and nine (twins), raised $150 with matching gifts from their parents and received a beautiful letter of appreciation from the director of the Children's Department. The president of the library is a friend of mine, and he was so impressed with the success of these children's fund-raiser that he hopes it will catch on in other families, because $150 can buy a lot of children's books.

The more satisfied we are with our lives, the more generous we tend to become. Giving back is always a good thing, and when you give to others, you gain enormous benefits as your life unfolds, whether you know it or not. What did your parents teach you about giving? What do you want to teach your children? What sort of giving do your children like to do? The earlier they understand altruistic giving, the more they will do to unselfishly serve others.

Good people have an innate instinct to be useful and do the right thing. We feel an obligation to ourselves to give back because it feels right to show our appreciation and gratitude. We become good at giving back through experience. The mere act of generosity is the reward; we do good because it makes us feel good. My brother had his children paint some of their extra bikes red and gave them to less fortunate children. Recently, Peter and I heard of a brave local nine-year-old girl who received an $11,000 award from the Make-A-Wish foundation, and it made us happy to learn about the opportunity to make a donation to help her wish come true. We are all parts of the universal good, and by acting with humanity we come to understand that the deed is what's important. It is its own reward.

When you truly feel compassion for others or feel richly blessed by their goodness, you naturally respond by wanting to help out. Rather than ask, "What can I do?" it is better to do something specific or offer a service. If neighbors lose power in a hurricane and your house has electricity, you can take them some hot soup and bread. You can offer to let them do their laundry at your home or use a spare room in order to have Internet access.

What sort of giving do you do? For years we've opened up our house for a kitchen tour to raise money for the Child & Family Agency of Southeastern Connecticut. Friends open their gardens to the public to raise funds for community projects. To raise money for the library after the storm, people in Stonington hosted dinner parties in their homes. Peter and I donated eight thousand books to China and Africa for literacy programs when we moved to Connecticut.

Nicholas, Anna, and Lily had a shelter golden retriever they dearly loved that died when they were very young. The loss hit Lily the hardest.

Once when we were walking their new golden, Homer, Lily pointed up to a gloriously puffy white cloud. "Big Mommy" (that's what she calls me), she said, "that is Carter, when he was a puppy." And, indeed, the cloud was in the shape of a beautiful golden retriever puppy. When the grandchildren have birthday parties, because of their love of dogs, they ask their friends not to give them presents but to make a donation to the animal shelter or to a program for the homeless. They have raised a lot of money, and their proud grandparents are always happy to contribute to their causes.

Of course, I become weak-kneed over how compassionate my grandchildren are at such young ages. They seem to have an innate desire to connect and give to others. I am a witness to their sense of sharing, and their parents have always stressed the importance of their working as a team. They look out for one another, and support each other in their collective values.

When I lived in New York City, I was on the board of an organization that provided food to the poor. Our church had a shelter caring for the homeless, and we provided support by spending the night. When I was the host of the HGTV show *Homes Across America*, I helped build a house for a family as part of Habitat for Humanity. I was proud to wear a hard hat and goggles and energetically pound those nails into the wood that would become a wall of a house for a family in need.

A friend who is a nurse drives one of her elderly former patients to his doctors' appointments, and on their way home they stop at a local restaurant for lunch. Her son is a chef, and he cooks supper for this man two nights a week.

Our dear friend Matt, a navy officer who served as a pilot in Iraq for four years, is now involved in caring for the Wounded Warriors. He and his wife, Kerri, host fund-raisers in their home in New Hampshire. A local restaurant, the Dog Watch Cafe, has a turkey drive every November. When customers give money, the owners of the cafe match the donation to provide turkeys for needy families' Thanksgiving dinners. The same restaurant also gives a discount to police and firefighters who come for a meal.

We have friends who informally adopted a teenage girl from a dysfunctional family, providing a stable home life and positive role models. A father of two avid lacrosse players wanted to do something for their coach and invited him and his wife to join them for a long weekend vacation at their time-share beach cottage in Bermuda.

Every Thursday morning our neighbor takes an elderly bachelor to buy his groceries. On their way, they stop for coffee at a favorite spot and have a relaxed visit. We have friends who counsel boys in jail. A friend who loves photography takes pictures of people who are donating their time for charity events and writes press releases for the newspapers about various fund-raisers.

Out of the blue, last winter a friend brought over a pair of mountain walking sticks for Peter in order for him to feel secure in the snow and ice of winter. There are angels who come and shovel our snow, straighten out our flag, drive us in bad weather, bring the recycling bin inside our gate on Tuesday mornings when we are out for breakfast.

Whether you and your family get involved with environmental cleanup at a local park or playground, or remove graffiti, or donate household items to a thrift shop and then offer to organize them, the most rewarding way to give back is to not have any expectations of benefit to you for your service. When you give from the pure, unadulterated goodness of your heart, everything you do will come back to you abundantly. The more you give away of your personal resources, the more wealthy your soul will be.

Peter and I like to give relief to unknown others. When we learn of a natural disaster somewhere in the world, it makes us feel better to send money to a relief fund. Sometimes we give to people we know, and we're glad we can help out with a specific need, but often we give anonymously. A friend told me that her late husband, Ralph, was the most generous man she'd ever known. He always made a point of giving money without letting the source of his gift be known to the recipient. His favorite cause was homeless shelters, where the need is so great.

I strongly believe that charity should begin at home; parents' examples of selflessness are such lessons to their children. So many parents tirelessly give of their resources to help their children succeed in academic life and sports, helping out at their schools, driving them to their practices and games, coaching Little League; their example will be vital to their children's entire development.

When I was a little girl, my father taught Sunday school in Southport, Connecticut. Every Easter the Episcopal bishop of Connecticut came to Trinity Church to give a sermon and every child was given a hyacinth plant. Children lined up to shake the bishop's firm (ouch) hand and receive a plant and a "Happy Easter."

After I grew up and moved to New York City, and eventually married Peter, I quietly arranged each year for four hundred hyacinth plants to be delivered to our Fifth Avenue church the day before Easter. Young Alexandra and Brooke kept the secret year after year and loved to help me tie colorful ribbons around the terra-cotta pots, a tradition we cherished together.

It feels wonderful to spontaneously give back to those who have been helpful to us and our communities. A friend baked cookies with her three children, and the whole family took them—and some bourbon—to the local police and fire departments late Christmas afternoon to thank their police officers and firefighters for all their care. The family sang a few carols, including "We Wish You a Merry Christmas." So sweet. We have a doctor friend in New York City who goes to hospitals every Christmas Day with his wife to visit the children, believing this makes the message of this holiday so meaningful. Our good friend Kerri, Matt's devoted wife and mother of four, told me with a chuckle, "I've found my purpose in life: serving others."

Neuroscientists have found that the act of helping another person activates the parts of the brain that are involved with pleasure and reward. The benefits you receive from serving others become biological. When we do good, we are rewarded by feeling good.

The best way to build good character is to do good deeds. We should consciously think of all we owe to others, and remember how caring, loving, and kind people have been to us. Let the words *sympathy, compassion, empathy, cooperation,* and *collaboration* guide our minds as we continue to find ways to give back.

Give of yourself and you will be good. When you are good, you will be living the good life. The whole earth is ours to enjoy, and while we have life we can take pleasure in giving benefits to others and feel the great sense of being part of the general good of the world.

Do all the good you can,
By all the means you can,
In all the ways you can,
At all the times you can,
To all the people you can,
As long as ever you can.

—John Wesley

18

....

Be Strong

Study something, learn something,
risk more than you think you can,
care something, become something.

—Michael Drury

We start with ourselves, and then, when we have taken care of ourselves appropriately, we're in a position of strength and knowledge to be useful to others. Until this truth is grasped, women will never be free to make anything of themselves or make a contribution of lasting value to the world.

Mothers and daughters both need to train themselves in self-sufficiency.

One of my fans, a journalist, wrote a review of my book *Things I Want My Daughters to Know,* and her remarks were quite glowing until she wrote about my essay "Think of Yourself: By Being Self-Centered, You May Be Benefiting the World." This writer thought I was off base and selfish. But I feel more strongly now than ever about women being able to take care of themselves and, no matter how difficult it is, carving out the necessary time to try to better understand themselves in order to have the strength of mind to rely on themselves if need be. (Of course this is equally true of men.)

Women must accept the fact that they might, at any moment, be alone. Accidents happen. Marriages fall apart. Illness occurs. Not all stories have happy endings. The great truth is that we have to always expect the unexpected. We should expect the best but be prepared for the worst. Life is mysterious, and unanticipated, often unthinkable situations do arise. It is true, I think, that one human instinct is to find someone to lean on. Share, yes; lean, no. We have to train our minds to be self-reliant.

A female minister friend and I were having a stimulating conversation about the reasons women are twice as depressed as men. Wendy's conclusion was that most women put themselves last. They are nurturers, like nurses; they put everyone else first and don't seem to get around to themselves. When Wendy counsels women parishioners, she hears of all the traditional roles women are expected to play. But many of the women she talks with have no interest in these roles, or worse, feel anxious, misunderstood, and depressed when participating in them.

Edward Burke talked about "an enlightened self-interest." I want nothing less than that for my daughters, and men *and* women all over the world. My sources of pleasure are different now from what they were twenty years ago. I avoid the negative energy that results from failing to care for my intellectual and emotional needs. Not only do I refuse to try to please everyone but I know my limitations. There are some activities I don't want to do, and my short answer when asked to do them is *no*. I really don't have to explain. I smile and laugh. No. And then I say, "No, thank you."

The shape and substance of your life can't be solely determined by the needs or desires of others. We have to learn to be unavailable to our spouses, our children, and our friends regularly in order to put our best selves in order. We should keep our focus on what we are trying to accomplish in our brief life span.

Mothers with young children should rely on babysitters, neighbors, friends, and nannies in order to be freed up to take care of their own well-being and affairs. Both Alexandra and Brooke value regularly having others spend time caring for their children in order for them to work. It is healthy for children to have other influences besides their parents. My daughters experienced a number of different caregivers while growing up and became quite attached to some of them. The world is their teacher, and children don't feel abandoned when they are not always under the thumb and guidance of their mothers and fathers. Quite the contrary. When a child is loved, she finds it fun to have a variety of caregivers who are playful and love to teach. These caregivers are older friends, and children can never have enough friends.

Life is paradoxical. The more we want to help others, the more we have to spend time away from them so that they can explore things on their own and develop self-confidence and self-trust. And the same is true for us. No one should lean on someone else more than she relies on herself. If you are diminished, what you can give to others is diminished. We must develop the strength to be able to be independently true to ourselves.

None of us are 100 percent indispensable. Mothers and wives may be essential and necessary, and heaven knows we can be useful; but if we're always on call, we are taken advantage of, and we know in our hearts that we are weakening, not strengthening, the character and independence of our loved ones. In your absence, things won't be done to your exacting standards, and yet, you can be thankful you weren't there for everyone else's continuous demands.

Center yourself. Be aware at all times of all that is in your control. Self-interest is *not* selfish; this is enlightenment! I believe in individualism; our primary responsibilities are self-reliance and personal responsibility. When a friend turned fifty, she realized she was leaning too much on her two sons, who are in college. Technology has made it so easy to communicate, but she understands she needs to be in less frequent contact so they can live their own lives more independently.

Live for yourself. Begin with yourself. This is who you are. The love you have for a husband or a child will be more authentic and genuine if you are as careful about the way you nurture yourself as you are about how you take care of others.

The sooner we face the reality that we raise children in order that they might grow up and leave us to explore vast opportunities all over the world, and not worry about what their mother will do without them, the happier and healthier we will all be.

Perhaps we try to live just for our husbands. But this puts inappropriate pressure on them. And it is wise to be able to live for and by yourself when you might find yourself alone someday, if you're fortunate enough to grow old. It is never too early to envision yourself, day to day, living by yourself. You don't have to be afraid, because when you no longer have others who depend on you, you'll be able to live with expansive freedom.

Love never dies. You shouldn't feel guilty about living for yourself after your husband dies. You'll be free to fill your world with your own interests and spend more time being self-fulfilled. Be prepared. Your goal should be to be strong when circumstances are beyond your control.

While we are still young, we should evaluate our inner resources. How happy are you when you are alone? How much do you value solitude? What do you find yourself wanting to do more of? What do you most love to do when you escape your responsibilities to others? What are some areas of study you want to explore? Where do you want to travel? If you found yourself alone, would you move? Where?

I suggest that while you're still in the thick of life and don't have the luxury of time on your hands, you begin to prepare yourself for a future time when you might no longer have the regular companionship of your intimate loved ones, when you must try to continue loving your life and find your private world fulfilling and happy.

Spending some reflective time soul-searching now could make your older years more rewarding and the transition into them smoother. The future will not be the same as the past, but it can and should be richly lived. I intend to set a good example to my daughters by thriving in my mature years.

The living self has one purpose only: to come into its own fullness of being.

—*D. H. Lawrence*

19

Do This for You

*Geniuses are the luckiest of mortals because what they must do is the
same as what they want to do and, even if their genius is unrecognized in
their lifetime, the essential earthly reward is always theirs, the certainty
that their work is good and will stand the test of time.*

—W. H. Auden

We humans are creative animals. Not only do we think, but we can
cause something to exist. We're capable of producing something original and good.

What we need is passion. Everyone should have some part of their
life that they can pursue with passion. The more, the better. We need to
feel powerful emotions in order to create something. I completely believe
that nothing great is ever achieved without enthusiasm. In order to do
anything well, we have to love what we're doing and believe in ourselves
whether others do or not. Even though there is all that other stuff in your
life, make sure that you have passions in your life at all times.

Whatever sacrifices you make, believe your efforts are worthwhile and will make a difference. Always have faith in the power of your love for what you are doing. When you are excited, your work will make your life interesting.

There are some unique contributions only you can make, and if you don't exert yourself, the work you could achieve will not exist because no one else has your visionary talent. Self-expression, achieving originality through creative effort and having your own point of view, is exciting, and exhilaration comes from your commitment to your chosen work.

Self-knowledge and self-confidence are essential; if we don't believe that what we are trying to do with our lives is meaningful, we will easily become discouraged and not be able to move ahead with our unique visions. When we are self-motivated, we realize we can't rush—we have to let our thoughts have space around them. Our belief in the integrity of what we are attempting to accomplish will make all the difference. You and I are not alone in our struggles, but we must be alone to concentrate our energies in rewarding ways.

What are some of the things you most love to do? Do you feel you have found your passions? What do you do for yourself that brings you your greatest happiness? What steps are you taking to spend more time engaging in activities you are passionate about without neglecting the other, necessary parts of your life? What kinds of sacrifices are you willing to make in order to have more boundless enthusiasm for the things that you are most passionate about?

Try to give birth to what you want to do and not to worry about being rejected. I am no stranger to rejection. I have zero regrets about creating work I believe in, and I have the enormous satisfaction of having made the effort, giving the work my all, and trying. It's natural to want to be appreciated for our talent. But recognition is far from automatic. What's essential for me, and I trust for you, is to make an earnest attempt, and be faithful in the mental exertion. Life's journey is a process of self-discovery, and when we learn more about the kinds of activities that excite us, we will become more inner-directed and understand that the real reward is in our effort to remain true to this core knowledge.

Just as death is a natural part of life, failure is a part of success. We all have to experiment, try new ways of expression, do research, and make new discoveries. Starting and finishing a project are equally painful. We have self-doubts, have a tendency to delay tackling a difficult task, and fool ourselves through procrastination. We just need to begin. Then once we're inside the work, it envelops us and completely takes us over, and we don't want the end to come, even though the deadline is staring us in the face. We know from bitter experience that the ending snuffs out the fire. It's all over. Nothing lasts forever. What could possibly be more fulfilling than to do work that is noble and that you love?

I often think of the English historian Edward Gibbon, the first volume of whose brilliant book *The History of the Decline and Fall of the Roman Empire* was published in 1776 (the year our cottage was built), and who suffered from a deep depression after he finished this important manuscript. When Peter left a copy of this book on an airplane by error, he bought another one and read it for a second time. It was that good. When you find your passion and when you're doing something meaningful and personally rewarding, the pleasure is in the process, not the finishing.

When Peter wrote a conclusion to his recent book *Figure It Out: A Guide to Wisdom*, he reflected: "I'm somewhat saddened to find myself writing down this final page of my manuscript, *Figure It Out*, that I began with some humility and trepidation over half a century ago . . ." He kept working on his book, hour after hour, adding, editing, eliminating, and all that work was so stimulating and satisfying. He saw no urgency to give it up. It was my encouraging him to show his manuscript to a publisher that led him to mail it off, and now, of course, he is so pleased it is out there, being read and appreciated.

There is no more wonderful feeling than to love what you do. If we're able to influence, help, and even inspire others with the results of our passions, that is a bonus. The work we choose to do should fuel our passion, and it is this energy that gives us the powerful drive necessary to exert ourselves, making a strenuous effort to bring out the best that's in us. The most pivotal moments in our lives are the times when we discover new, exciting ideas that make us passionate. I raised my daughters with the advice to never sell their souls. I believe I set an excellent example for Alexandra and Brooke by being passionate about my work and my life. I feel that our mother-daughter relationships have been strengthened because I have faithfully remained true to myself and have thoroughly enjoyed whatever work I chose to pursue. I'm grateful that both my daughters reach out for their best life possible.

Believe that with your feelings and your work you are taking part in the greatest; the more strongly you cultivate this belief, the more will reality, and the world, go forth from it.

—Rainer Maria Rilke

20

···

Use Your Imagination, Remember, and Travel

Because they have so little, children must rely on imagination rather than experience.

—Eleanor Roosevelt

Wouldn't it be wonderful if we were endowed with unusual foresight and didn't have to learn our life lessons too late, by hindsight? Going inside our souls, formulating a mental image of something not real or present, is what human beings are capable of excelling in; we're able to bring things into existence. Imagination is what is possible when we give ourselves the gift of solitude. Everyone who is able to think is able to visualize, to call something to mind, and to imagine.

When we think up a plan, we are bringing something out of, or through, our minds. The human mind is divine. Ask yourself, what is the most exciting thing you can think about in this exact moment? Now, this very second, is when you set your mind on fire and imagine something that will inspire you.

Everything we do begins in the imagination. Our inner space will inspire the best in us when we give ourselves the essential time and quiet, away from the pressures or influences of others. We are in charge of how we put our imaginations to productive use because only we, as human beings, can create.

We must deliberately will our imaginations toward our desired goals, and we learn from experience that our imaginations grow when we keep our minds in sharp focus. Imagination can't be rushed or forced; it must be brought out into the light. There is no greater life force than imagination. When we have the creative powers of our minds, through trial and error, dedicated self-awareness, and discipline we will feel most alive and will be happiest.

We arrive at the understanding and discovery of truth through our imaginations. Einstein, who worshiped his imagination, figured out that the most incomprehensible thing about the universe is that it is comprehensible. Through our imaginations, we will be able to communicate authentically and feel a deep sense of satisfaction in the creative process.

Keep your sense of childhood playfulness alive. The answers to the mysteries are somewhere for us to uncover. Feel the enlivening of your spirit through your fertile imagination. Think of all the exciting places you can go, the people you can see, and the things you can do. I guarantee you will never be bored when you tap into this divine human resource, your imagination. Never lose sight of the power of your imagination to remember the most extraordinary events in your mind and life. Don't dull life down as you mature.

We will remember best the happiest moments in our lives, as well as the saddest times. We tend to forget the mundane. Why is it that there are some tragic moments that, no matter how hard we try, we *cannot* forget? The answer is that we reinforce them over and over, and they become indelible in our brains. We remember our most deeply felt emotional experiences. Our memories are our autobiographies. We won't remember everything, good or awful, but we can remember all the beautiful memories by recalling them often.

Try not to give in to forgetfulness. You can work to improve your memory so that it will make you, and your friends and family, happy. Never admit to having a poor memory. No one remembers everything. If some things are not important to you, you won't remember them. As long as they're written down somewhere, you can know what you need to know.

I believe in selective memory. I want to fill my mind with life-enhancing, positive, beautiful memories. The dark experiences can remain buried without a funeral. Take the good in your life and run with it in your memory, and when you desire to imagine all the wonderful things possible in a human life, your memories will inspire excellence because you choose to focus on what's best and what brings you your greatest happiness.

I've found that when I write something down, I tend to remember it better. When we have the attitude that we want to accentuate the positive, we must write down only the things we want to remember and let the others be buried in the sands of time. If I find myself dwelling on a memory that is upsetting, I go for a vigorous walk to clear my head. We have it in our power to choose how we relate to life's blows. Our attitude is everything.

I want to continue to imagine, remember, and travel. I've learned that the more I travel and reach out to new, exciting adventures, the greater my meaningful, life-sustaining memories. When I'm not on a vacation, I hold the memories of favorite places in my mind and imagination as I anticipate places I dream I will explore.

Peter shares my love of Paris. I feel blessed we both value this place we hold so dear that supports our happiest memories. Many people have never been to Paris, and if they did go, it is possible they would not love it as we do. It is not important to go to Paris; Paris is symbolic. It is really about doing what is in your heart. Traveling to Paris is not possible or appropriate for everyone. Each of us has to find *our* Paris—a place we love that holds our hearts, where we feel comfortable and happy. Do not be afraid to grasp yours.

Each of my daughters has found her Paris: Brooke's Paris *is* Paris, France, and has been since her first visit, when she was five. For now, Alexandra's Paris is a beautiful deserted beach. What's most important is to have a place you love to go to in real life as well as in your imagination and memories that brings you great joy.

Whether we travel in our minds or in reality, we can hold up in our consciousness the essential tools of using our imaginations, our ability to remember, and our passion to travel and always seek new adventures.

Eureka!

—Archimedes

21

··

Don't Go Through Life,
Grow Through Life—
Be Unafraid of Change

Difficulties are meant to rouse, not discourage.
The human spirit is to grow strong by conflict.

—*William Ellery Channing*

We evolve, and it is appropriate to change our minds throughout our lives. Nothing, as we know, ever stays the same. It is up to us to accept reality and, in the light of truth, act appropriately. Trust yourself to know when the time is right, and then act.

When we're blessed with reasonable health and are likely to have the privilege of growing old, our values have to change in order for us to make this final, significant phase of our lives transformative. We can achieve changes for the better only when we accept that we have evolved and our values have changed. To change our thoughts in changed circumstances is wisdom.

Peter and I are heartened to discover how sensitive and thoughtful Brooke and Alexandra are to us as we mature. As they evolve, they are not only recipients but also great givers of wisdom.

Having my own garden early in life made me aware that life is an evolving process. Everything that is alive undergoes continuous growth. We need to feel free to invent and reinvent ourselves throughout our lives. We retire from one activity in order to keep growing. We give up what we did earlier in our lives to create time and space to do something else.

By letting go of parts of our former lives, we're free to reinvent the wheel. My having given up being an interior designer allows me to spend my days studying. I needed to start over and challenge myself. Winston Churchill understood that we must continuously make an effort. He said, "Never, never, never give up" and "I have nothing to offer but blood, toil, tears and sweat." Churchill, late in life, took up painting and became quite a good artist.

Years ago when a silver company launching their china and crystal collection asked me to design a table setting, I went the extra mile. Rather than selecting a tablecloth, I used my passion for ribbons to inspire me to weave ribbons together in shades of purple, yellow, and green, with pansy flowers as the centerpiece and color inspiration. My display was a success, and a fabric company, seeing the exhibition, put my design in their line called Le Ribbon in five different colorways. I had a seamstress make matching sundresses in different colors for Alexandra, Brooke, and me. It was great fun.

In the 1970s, the international fabric company Scalamandré Silk asked me to color some eighteenth-century hand-screened textiles from their archives. Always up for an exciting challenge, I took some black-

and-white drawings and colored them, each with several different color-ways; some of these old print designs had up to thirty-three different screens, making my assignment stimulating, to say the least. During the months I worked on this project, in my dreams, words became colors!

At the same time, Scalamandré had me create a collection called Giverny, named for Monet's garden, for which I designed original color schemes from many of their existing fabrics. When this assignment worked out well, I realized afresh how important it is to dare to try something new.

The more I study the masters and sages, the ancient classical thinkers, and all who learned from those before them, the more prepared I feel to greet life's hurdles. As I continue to develop in my maturity, I experience a more expansive intensity that supports my growth.

The fact that life is difficult doesn't in any way mean we can't celebrate the good times fully, without guilt or superstitious worry that troubles lie ahead. We should deal with an absolute understanding of life's nature, preparing ourselves in the best way we can to be realistic about how much effort and hard work goes into excellence and living well. The happiness that results from our hard work is an achievement, not something automatic. Happiness graces us when we do our best with our talents, reach far and wide for opportunities, and meet whatever challenges are unavoidable.

When I was in my thirties and forties, I felt sorry for old people, but this was due to my ignorance. When we accept life as it comes and continue to grow, all our years of experiences accumulate to give us more pleasurable moments because we truly know what is most important in life—love and friends.

It takes a long time to grow up. We want to be worthy of our self-respect. The gradual evolution toward being the people we want to become takes place every hour of our lives. As we make steady progress in understanding life's purpose, our lives will become deeply meaningful and fulfilling.

Why stay we on earth except to grow?

—*Robert Browning*

22

....

Make Healthy Choices
About Food and Money

A wise man should consider that health
is the greatest of human blessings.

—Hippocrates

Wouldn't it be wonderful if we could eat whatever we wished to, whenever we wanted to, and still stay healthy? Wouldn't it be grand if we could spend as much money as we chose to and our bank accounts would never be depleted? Dream on.

We need to eat to stay alive. Sadly, our culture is now addicted to cheap, fake, hyperprocessed foods. Michael Pollan, in his book *Food Rules: An Eater's Manual*, wrote intelligently about what we should eat. Some of my favorite food rules are

- *Don't eat anything your great-grandmother wouldn't recognize as food.*

- *Avoid food products that contain more than five ingredients.*
- *Avoid foods you see advertised on television.*
- *Eat foods made from ingredients that you can picture in their raw state or growing in nature.*
- *Eat only food that has been cooked by humans.*
- *Eat well-grown food from healthy soil.*
- *The whiter the bread, the sooner you'll be dead.*

Everyone's metabolism is different. Meat has sustained humanoids for tens of thousands of years, and while a good case can be made, at least environmentally, for vegetarianism—where you eat vegetables, grains, fruits, nuts and seeds, but no meat—this diet may not be right for everyone. Eating well for your health, your weight, the planet, and animals is a choice only you can make.

I believe that in order to live well, we must eat well. I love food and laughingly tell people I've never missed a meal. But I think we should do our homework and educate ourselves about the connection between what we want to eat and what is healthiest for us to eat. The research is out there, and it is compelling. While my daughters don't entirely share my beliefs about food, they are respectful of the path Peter and I have embraced.

Just as we have to choose the food we and our families eat, we have to come to grips with our finances. We can't afford to run out of money. Other than the cost of the travel that I consider a real priority, my daily life's expenses are relatively simple. Lao Tzu taught us, "There is no calamity greater than lavish desires. There is no greater guilt than discontentment. And there is no greater disaster than greed."

We have to earn more than we spend. Period. Money doesn't come from thin air any more than babies come from a stork. If you're in debt, work out a plan to become debt-free as soon as possible, even if it requires sacrifice and pain. Watch your dollars carefully. Keep good monthly records in order to be able to compare your status from year to year. You need to be aware of income versus cash flow. Don't expect others to bail you out. Everyone who cares about being self-sufficient will put themselves on a budget and have a systematic plan of specific sums of money allocated for particular purposes.

If you are debt-free and have your finances in order, the weaker members of society, whether in your own family or in other nations, will seek your help. We all need to be careful not to give more than is appropriate, otherwise the domino effect drags us all down. Peter, because he was raised during the deep Depression, has a tendency to preserve money rather than to spend it.

You cannot be too careful with your money. Look for the hidden fees. Read the fine print. Peter and I gave up credit cards that charged random fees at the end of the bill, or fees for late payments when we hadn't received the bill. We had difficulty canceling the credit cards. It certainly is easier to get into something than to get out of it. By being meticulous about your finances, you won't have to go through life hand-to-mouth. Each one of us has to earn our own living. If you're willing to work hard, you are entitled to spend the money you earn however you wish. You deserve to reap the benefits of your own efforts and good fortune. If we can teach our children and our grandchildren to have a strong work ethic and to know the value of a dollar, they will be free to live within their means and enjoy whatever blessings come to them without the crushing burden of debt.

Good friends came to spend time with us in Stonington on a brilliantly sunny, crisp day with no humidity. We drove down to the beach at the end of Water Street and silently watched a magnificent sunset. Love, friendship, and nature's beauty are priceless gifts we shared in abundance. We were feeling particularly blessed in our lives that glorious day, and before our friends drove back to New Hampshire, one of them gave Peter a piece of paper with a smile. It said, "If you want to feel rich, count all the things in your life that money can't buy" (author unknown).

As Mark Twain clearly knew, "To be satisfied with what one has: that is wealth." What a wealth of advice. Lesson number one: Feel and appreciate the abundance of your own resources because trust in yourself creates your well-deserved wealth. I can't help repeating myself about this point. The last entry in Peter's book *Figure It Out* is a quotation of William Ellery Channing, words Peter has tucked in his wallet. It begins: "To live content with small means; to seek elegance rather than luxury, and refinement rather than fashion; to be worthy, not respectable, and wealthy, not rich . . ."

We will be wealthy when we know how to take care of our necessities and we've learned when enough is enough. How we eat and how we handle our money are delicate topics. Go gently on others. If you are a convert to a new diet, try not to proselytize. Everyone has to change from one way of thinking and behaving to another on their own terms, in their own time. No matter how much someone tries to persuade us, we have to be ready to embrace the information before their persuasion will take effect. When we have a healthy attitude about the food we choose to eat and the way we manage our money, we will be wise and free to live fully and well.

I don't feel any need to discuss food and money with my daughters because I believe they are managing their affairs splendidly; they are both health conscious, and, while they eat a more Western diet than Peter and I do, they make healthy choices and keep well informed about food and nutrition. Alexandra and Brooke enjoy eating a lot of fruit, vegetables, and salads, and so do their children.

Because meals are so central to our time together as a family, I would never choose to make my daughters or grandchildren feel self-conscious about what they put into their mouths just because I don't eat many of the things that they do. It took me roughly sixty-eight years to evolve into the diet I feel most comfortable with, and I am the last person to judge what other people choose to eat.

Just as we don't discuss food—other than to rave about something we're enjoying—the subject of money rarely comes up in our family unless one of my daughters insists on treating us to dinner or buys us a gift. Because they both have far more access to retail moments, they find ideal presents for Peter and me, and I often want to reimburse them because they are acting as intelligent, informed personal shoppers.

As their mother, I feel blessed by the way my daughters handle their financial responsibilities—for instance, being realistic about education expenses for their children. I'm also grateful that both Alexandra and Brooke encourage Peter and me to continue to travel; somehow their blessing sweetens our experience.

Wealth is not without its advantages and the case to the contrary, although it has often been made, has never proved widely persuasive.

—John Kenneth Galbraith

23

....

Value Time, Don't Deny Death, and Grow Old Vigorously

Hold fast the time! Guard it, watch over it, every hour, every minute!
Unregarded it slips away . . . Hold every moment sacred.
Give each clarity and meaning, each the weight of . . . awareness,
each its time and due fulfillment.

—Thomas Mann

One of the kindest, most generous ways of showing love and affection is to not be needy of other people and, worse, be demanding of their time. No one has ever *seen* time, but it is what we use to order our lives. In my book *Time Alive* I asked my readers, "What do you choose to do with the 8,766 hours a year each of us has to work with and use productively?" Time, as we know, is swift in its passage. It thrusts us forward with mathematical regularity, whether we've paid attention or not.

The best gift parents, teachers, and caregivers can give a child is time management skills. Time is the same for all of us, but not all of us know how to manage it well. Children are never too young to understand the priceless value of time, and they should be given the responsibility of making their own choices about how to best use their free time from early childhood.

We have the capacity for growth, we can develop and hone our skills, and we can discover and create great things when we understand how valuable time is to us. Everything we do is in some limited time frame; even if we go to a log cabin in the woods with no clock and read for five years, the rest of the world hears the clock tick by and time marches us into the unknown future.

At this stage in my life, I don't have the immediate responsibilities of a rigorous domestic life with the commitments and concerns involved with raising a family to squeeze every ounce of my time. I don't have a difficult boss who wants every last hour of my time. Without these constraints, one would assume I have nothing but time on my hands.

Not true. I am tough on myself. I resent anyone who wastes my time. I do not take time for granted. I know I won't live forever, and while I'm alive, I choose to thrive. I value every hour as it vanishes forever. I want to enjoy what I'm experiencing, and I like to feel a sense of accomplishment from the energy I put into the task at hand. I'm willing to work hard, and I like seeing good results. There *is* time if we learn not to waste it.

Now that Peter is ninety-one, I have become increasingly more discerning about what we do and what we do not do, because one never knows. I'm not sure I will ever come to the conclusion that I have "plenty of time," because I have projects that would take dozens of years to complete, but I do understand the value and virtue of living "in the moment" and, as Virginia Woolf believed, with this consciousness, moments can be "big as years."

When we are mindful of our present experience, we are valuing our time in a soulful way. Those with whom we elect to share our time will also benefit from our sensitive awareness. We have to train our minds to become completely absorbed in the reality of whatever is going on at the moment. This discipline automatically opens us up to a deeper, more profound intelligence and understanding that enables us to tap into our innate intuitive powers. And, in this awareness, we experience timelessness, a flow state of inner peace and intense enjoyment, with full awareness of being alive in the present.

Right now is the only time to live well; living can't be put off to some other time in the future. We can't afford to bank on anything that is unknown. The reality is that there really is no other time we can count on after this hour; we can make it our finest.

No matter what we've done in the past, that was where we were then. Each of us is different now. Over time we've had so many real life experiences and have evolved to now have fresh insights, and in many of our beliefs, we have a dissimilar point of view from the one we held previously.

The future takes me away from my present mindfulness. The future comes soon enough. Whoosh! I want to fill up time with awareness. I want moments to teach me something new. I want what I do with my time to prove appropriate, productive, and pleasant. The greater a value we place on each hour, the more authentically we live. Horace Mann wrote, "Lost, yesterday, somewhere between sunrise and sunset, two golden hours, each set with sixty diamond minutes. No reward is offered, for they are gone forever."

Wasting time makes us feel dull, bored, and useless. The Dhammapada, the body of teachings expounded by the Buddha, expresses this understanding well:

> *Few cross over the river. Most are stranded on this side. On the riverbank they run up and down. But the wise person, following the way, Crosses over, beyond the reach of death . . . Free from desire, Free from possessions, Free from attachment and appetite, Following the seven lights of awakening, And rejoicing greatly in his Freedom, In this world the wise person becomes themselves a light, Pure, shining, free.*

There's death in life and life in death, and there's some kind of life after death. The act of dying, when the soul moves out of the physical realm, when its energy moves on somewhere, somehow, is a natural, painless process. It is up to each one of us to continue to explore this mystery in our own way, on our own terms—because death is inevitable; everything that comes into being dies. I want to live as fully as my energy allows me, and at the same time, have as few regrets as possible when destiny calls.

As we grow older, it is our job to fulfill our obligations to ourselves, our families, and society, by paying attention to our bodies, our minds, and our actions. Falling apart, or giving up, is not a wise option. Most of us deny the inevitable, and as a consequence, we haven't sufficiently cultivated the inner resources necessary to shift the emphasis from how we look to who we are. It is exasperating when people are in denial about their age, going to extreme measures to try to stay "forever young." You can't stop aging, but you can dictate some of the terms of your aging process. A Gallup poll found that, by almost any measure, people get happier as they get older. The beauty of growing old is the sense of freedom you feel from not having to prove anything to anyone. You're in charge.

As we age, we must not dry up, shrivel, or droop. We don't want to lose our passion, our life force, our freshness, or reasons to live the good life. We must strive to continue to do things well, as we admire with awe the major accomplishments of those rare souls who excel and inspire us to stretch ourselves.

When we expend energy, it increases our energy. Movement is all. Always get dressed, even if you are not going outside. In order to continue to be enthusiastic about your life, at least once a year, plan an adventurous vacation far in advance. The research you do to prepare for the trip is educational, and the anticipation of your trip will give you a great deal of pleasure in the months leading up to your departure.

One of the most essential qualities of spirit as we grow old is gratitude. When we focus on all the wonderful people and experiences we've enjoyed, it lifts us up, and we don't spend our time being slumped in depression or complaining.

My message to my daughters is to never allow yourself to be over the hill. Keep on keeping on. Live to the hilt. Try to always live up to your highest potential. When you do, your satisfaction will be felt every moment you are alive. Never be an old person. Give yourself a break, and give everyone else one, too.

I rejoice in life for its own sake. Life is no brief candle to me. It is a sort of splendid torch which I've got to hold up for a moment and I want to make it burn as brightly as possible before handing it on to the future generations.

—George Bernard Shaw

24

....

Practice Patience

Patience and Diligence, like Faith, remove Mountains.

—William Penn

The ultimate wisdom is patience.

When we're patient, we have the capacity to put up with difficulties and tolerate delays and inconveniences without complaining. Patience emphasizes calmness and self-control. It's difficult to have trust and confidence in people who fly into a rage at the slightest provocation. When we're patient, we endure our fate. The anxious, restless, impatient person usually scowls in disapproval. On a purely practical note, while it may not be totally noble, it is nonetheless good to realize that impatience is an obvious character flaw and will make you feel awful about yourself. Michel de Montaigne believed we undo ourselves by our impatience. When we cultivate patience, we will remain in the middle, not overreacting to situations that come and go; nothing lasts, good or bad, pleasure or pain.

One of the gifts of growing older is our ability to endure, to bear with tolerance whatever the consequences. We're better able to carry on through our difficulties, no matter what the hardship or annoyance. Alexandra told me once that I have oceans of patience. I consider that a compliment because I have trained myself to be more tolerant and understanding.

When we are endlessly patient with a loved one, we are tapping into our inner strength; because this quality of excellence is a tangible way to show unconditional love. Patience provides an opportunity for gentle, kind, thoughtful, and often deeply tender interchange between loved ones.

Patience is a discipline. In order for me to stay in the breath, mindful of each moment, I light a candle that encourages calmness. I do a one-flower meditation, where I focus my energy on one living object to remind me that the beauty, color, and fragrance of a flower grew and blossomed in its own time. I've added patience to my daily meditation. When we practice patience, as in any other form of mindfulness, we will be persevering, faithful to the excellence of our character. Our patience is powerful. We're able to remain true to our highest powers. Patience is acceptance, and it gives us grace.

In order to live a mindful life, we have to take deep breaths, focus our awareness on our feelings, and come back to ourselves. In a moment of acting impulsively, ask yourself what your soul needs right now. When we're patient, we're self-controlled.

Keep living fully. Don't give in, but don't pretend. The best way I know to deal with the inevitability of aging is to value patience above all other virtues. I assure you, when you are patient, you'll be able to use all your vital energy positively. When you're patient, all of your moral virtues are at play.

I have a small bell on my writing desk that I randomly ring. I stop and, as mindfully as possible, focus on all the blessings in my life. Patience has taught me to concentrate on the love I feel in my heart, the love I share with others, and my love of life.

The key to practical wisdom is patience.

If there is one thing I wish to pass on to my daughters, it is the greatest virtue of all—patience. I'm now acutely aware of how patience can be life transforming. Once you learn to be patient, you will discover that it is very comforting and satisfying. You do whatever has to be done and march forward, one step at a time. It's really quite liberating. We must be realistic and accept what we cannot change.

Patience pays off over and over again, in every conceivable situation. Patience works because it feeds generosity, courage, and thoughtfulness, and encourages joy in a calm and understanding manner. What's remarkably powerful about patience is that it provides tender, positive, vivid experiences that can be savored.

I choose to be a reasonable, loving person, and I've made patience my trusted friend.

Be calm. Be patient. All is well and all will be well.

Genius is only a greater aptitude for patience.

—Georges-Louis Leclerc, Comte de Buffon

Acknowledgments

To Carl Brandt,

I'm grateful to the people in our lives who made it possible for you to become my literary agent.

Since 1974—after twenty-eight books—I value your judgment, intelligence, thoughtfulness, and friendship. You give generously of your talent and time to help me to be on the right path, for the right reason.

Your belief in me continues to inspire my work and brings me great happiness.

Love and appreciation,
Sandie

To Jessica McGrady,

Great thanks to you, my new superb editor, for doing a splendid editing job, sensitively respectful of my voice.

Your support about the title and subtitle means the world to me.

Special thanks to you for continuously reminding me how wonderful my family is.

With admiration, appreciation, and affection,
Alexandra

To my teachers,

Whatever wisdom I have acquired over the years has come from a combination of living and reading the works of philosophers and great thinkers.

The ones who have meant the most to me over the years are:

Aristotle
Michel de Montaigne
Ralph Waldo Emerson
René Dubos
Pierre Hadot